NORDIC *by* NATURE

gestalten | borderless

Foreword

by Andrea Petrini

Writer / food curator and
GELINAZ! co-founder

"Where are we now?" That was what David Bowie asked himself in the middle of *The Next Day*, just before approaching *Blackstar*, his cryptic recorded last testament about how life had been to him.

How has life been to us? And to the Nordic kitchen, we might add? Time is not ripe to announce, like Bowie, a distant future with a "goodbye" somewhere between the lines. Despite its worldwide accolades and recognition, time is tight. A reboot best be on its way.

Make no mistake: Nordic food has never seen better days. Everybody is buying their slice of cake. Youngsters are flocking by the hundreds to settle in Denmark, Sweden, Finland, Norway, and even in the remote wilderness of the Faroe Islands to start anew. You can't blame them. Those are the places to be. Look at the poor, brave Michelin guys forced at last to scout through the main Scandinavian capitals as if they were unspoiled lands they could declare their own, deciding which ones are bankable and which ones hard to sell. That is in their nature; judgmentalists at heart. Of course, they know how to do their jobs, and they sort of do it right. Which means: maybe they are missing the whole point.

The Nordic food scene is a win-win: everybody seems to get their share. Of course, historically speaking, it started out like a political statement. A Luther King thing, enacting freedom of speech for the scattered herd. A manifesto whose first revolutionary steps were to assemble the brave chefs who could position themselves outside of the usual framed and controlled languages, out from under the thumb of French, Italian, and Spanish idioms. They were outcasts. It was an exhilarating, intoxicating, liberating kick in those days, more than 13 years ago. But besides all that, beyond that Decalogue—a sort of straitjacket that seemed almost like an iron maiden—a brand new set of possibilities were unlocked.

Do less, get more. Look around and pick up ideas. Let nature be your muse. Know yourself and know your peers, scan and print your dreams in 3D. Play the game, don't forget to sign the postcard from home: all those blond, bearded Vikings and their beautiful companions and children caught among green hills and cascading waters. Cuisine has never found itself so close to nature.

But there's a life, an afterlife beyond what lies at close range, beyond what is commonly called "kitchen ring – the inner circle". Of course, expectations are high. Everybody is looking for a sign of things to come, of new roads to cross. With the hope of finally finding a clue to answer the question that everybody has been asking for years:

"What now? Where are we are now?"

Indeed.

To reboot itself, the Nordic kitchen needs new oxygen to fill its lungs, to pump up through its brain, to go beyond what's become predictable: the holy marriage of raw and wild, of astringency and "seaness," of granitic, austere root vegetables in the wintertime. What about going beyond the stereotypes, joyfully digging deeper in the unconscious mind, channeling back the rough Viking inside of you—this time in a gentler mood. A rounded, well-mannered, truer version of yourself, the gentleness of cooking, of getting to know you better—stating your claim with an exclamation mark.

Go back to studying, know your classics, invent your own history. Forget the usual storytelling, first things first: invent your own language. Here and now means what it literally means: the need to express the urgency of what lies in front of you. Transcend borders, put new formulas in motion day after day, test assumptions, ask questions, and make sure nobody can really provide the answers—because deep down inside, we all know that answers are much less important than the questions that precede them.

The moment a revolutionary becomes a bureaucrat and a passionate lover a husband, the risk of being predictable is almost a certainty. Embrace your commando mode: never expect anything to be taken for granted. Be fast and catch your own people off guard. Nordic cuisine is by far the most exciting thing to have happened on European soil in the last 15 years. Right from the start, it has been able to provide a framework, a common horizon, some sort of improvised heritage. It is time to diversify, to spread out. Everybody needs to sculpt their own identity. The tribe has scattered, each one tending his own field of language. Let the Vikings settle down, let them have wives, kids, and mortgages, and never forget the secret flame that burns inside each and every one of them.

Time is ripe to switch from politics to poetics. To speak in tongues, even. To be so unique, so unpredictable in your movements that not even your shadow can follow in your footsteps. I'll see you there, where no one has ever gone and where no one is expecting us. One little step further. No need for cars, no need for old tires. Yes, let's make the Michelin scouts sweat their shirts off: surely they need some exercise if they one day want to be able to handle everything that is coming their way? Let's get them—and everybody else—asking: "Where are we now?".

A trip across the North Atlantic and Arctic oceans. A 12-month, 5000-kilometer culinary exploration by land, air, and sea. Crushing through polar ice on Arctic fishing vessels and drifting through snowstorms on summer Michelin tires.

An Australian, a Swede, and two Danes—borderless by nature—embark on a journey throughout the great Kingdom of Denmark, from its vibrant inner city centers to the furthest-flung reaches of Greenland and the Faroe Islands. Circumnavigating the peninsula and archipelago of islands that form the "mainland" of Denmark and voyaging through the Kattegat and Danish straits that connect to the North and the dimly lit Baltic seas.

A trip first embarked through the early millennium by the pioneering Danish chef and the culinary entrepreneur who, to a great extent, would inspire the ideology behind the widening of food diversity in the Nordic region. A journey that would later formalize *Nordisk mad* (Danish for "Nordic food"), followed by the dogma commonly known today as "Nordic Cuisine"—uniting the nations, culinary customs, and climatic diversities of the Nordic region.

Fifteen years on, our voyage tracing the route of those intrepid culinary pioneers explores the evolution of Danish food culture since the reinvention, reinterpretation, and resurgence of the Nordic kitchen.

It is a resurgence driven by directional chefs to reinstate a rich diversity of locally sourced ingredients and traditions; to address the need for change in the homogeneous state of culinary culture and a spoiled landscape led by aggressive agro-business that has impacted domestic cuisine with disastrous effects.

Nordic by Nature documents the redrafting of Denmark's cultural culinary heritage.

This is not just a book, nor a collection of recipes. It is an inspirational insight into the state of the industry as a whole and a reflection of the revolutionary players who create it. The participants have been selected based on their relationship with regional, seasonal-based dining, their procurement of raw materials, and respect for the producer, chef, consumer and environment.

We want to feed the craving for the contemporary Danish kitchen with a collection of recipes crafted by the pioneers of this movement themselves; to form an authentic conjugate by capturing the enthusiasm of the chefs in their own kitchen; and to provide you, the reader, with the tools to reconstruct Denmark's contemporary culinary creations for your dining room table.

Encompassing personal stories and ideologies, failures, interpretations, foraging trips, and geographical and seasonal limitations (or possibilities!), all of which define this movement, *Nordic by Nature* features chefs' innovative recipes coupled with their own personal interpretation of the contemporary Danish kitchen. This is visualized through vibrant imagery of spaces, be it the kitchens, labs, forests, or castle gardens where inspiration is drawn, created, and consumed.

The dust has yet to settle. This is an admired moment in gastronomy, and this book aims to document and share this pivotal and inspirational shift in Danish gastronomy to serve as historical reference.

The chefs testify before nature, setting this book as the stage for the trial of the Nordic kitchen; here for you to witness, interpret, and recreate.

This curated work would not be complete without you, the learned reader. We hope it is as inspiring to you as the innovation and longevity of the Nordic kitchen is to us.

Borderless Co.
Not bound by geographical, nor cultural borders, a collective of curious individuals inspired by documenting original content.

Without limits: an intellectual curiosity that defines *borderless*.

Nordisk Mad
by Claus Meyer

I am from a country where ascetic doctors and puritan priests have led a 300-year-long anti-hedonistic crusade against the pleasure-giving qualities of food and against sensuality as such. For centuries in Denmark, the idea of preparing wonderful meals for your loved ones was considered a sin, in line with theft, abuse of alcohol, exaggerated dancing, incest, and masturbation. The philosophy so successfully communicated by these fine people was, that if you wanted to live a long life of health and prosperity on earth and avoid going to hell, what you needed to do is to eat something with inferior taste and get it over with in a hurry.

It was in this spirit that I was raised, in a middle-class family in the sixties, the darkest period in Danish food history. In my family, food had to be cheap and it had to be prepared and eaten in a maximum of 30 minutes.

My mother Ulla represented the first generation of Danish women who worked outside the home. Her luck was that this was the era of the stock cube, sauce colouring, canned meatballs, potato powder and steaks in a tin.

Industrial, chopped fatty meat of the cheapest possible quality and frozen vegetables pre-boiled years before they were consumed were the staples of my childhood. Everything was stocked in massive chest freezers in our basement. After being thawed, the meat would be wrapped in toasted bread crumbs three to four times before being deep-fried in margarine packed with trans fatty acids. Every night my mother would melt 500 grams (1 cup) of margarine for the three of us and whatever was left after frying was used for dipping. The most common sauce in my childhood was melted margarine. At the age of 14 I weighed 97 kilograms (213 pounds) and I was amongst the three fattest kids in southern Denmark.

Eating in my childhood was never a matter of reaching out for the beauty of life—it was a matter of economic efficiency.

Those formative years spent in culinary darkness were contrasted by one year spent in the culinary paradise of Agen, the capital of Gascony, in France. A year that radically changed my life.

I experienced for the first time in my life the fact that food could be beautiful and spiritual.

In France, I saw that there was a better way of producing food, grounded in ideas like diversity, seasonality, deliciousness, and connectedness to the land. I wanted people to open their hearts and minds to the virtues of food and cooking. Coming from a divorced family, I longed for what I saw in France: beautiful meals with the whole family sitting around the table for hours. I had come to believe that if only you could get food right, it would solidify some of the most important social structures in everyday life. Maybe it would fix love.

Guy, the chef, with whom I lived in Agen–and with his wife–had taught me that "happiness, my son, is about knowing what you want to do with your life, and having the guts to follow your heart."

So, at the age of 21 I returned to Denmark with a calling. I wanted to change the food culture of my country. After university and for something like a decade I felt like I ran around like a maniac trying, almost single-handedly, to repair the vast array of imperfections in food culture constantly stumbled upon. I managed this with a certain success, yes, but with very limited impact.

In 2001, I came to the conclusion that it would probably be more effective to take a top-down approach to the concept of transforming our food culture, at least at the beginning. When I contributed to a book about modern Spanish cuisine I got to meet some of the greatest Spanish chefs and learned that in 1973 they had set out to change their cuisine and hell, now 25 years later Spain was widely considered the ruling culinary destination in the world. This inspiration was coupled with influences drawn from the subtleties of Danish Dogma film makers, who in the late nineties under the leadership of Lars von Trier launched their manifesto that for more than a moment, at least in Europe, changed the dynamics of film making. Influenced by these incidents, with a small group of collaborators I started flirting with the idea that maybe one day a revitalized Nordic cuisine could be counted amongst the greatest in the world. At least, we were unable to see why not.

The timing seemed right: French cuisine had lost momentum and Spanish cuisine that had been almost undisputedly celebrated for the previous 10 years had increasingly alienated itself from nature, leaning toward molecular gastronomy and a somewhat less "organic" avenue toward deliciousness.

Eventually, we decided to do two things, the first was to open a restaurant, Noma, its name a portmanteau of the two Danish words *Nordisk* (Nordic) and *mad* (food). It would explore ancient Nordic cooking techniques and try to invent new ones, while working solely with local produce, which at the time was an outrageous idea.

I onboarded a young chef, René Redzepi, as the head chef and offered him a partnership. In the very first menu of Noma, back in 2003, we wrote that with this restaurant we wanted to create a New Nordic Cuisine that embraces the Arctic and brightens the world by virtue of its great taste and unique character.

Noma was never really meant to be the best restaurant in the world. Our aim was to explore the potential of our own territory and to inspire chefs to be a driving force in a transformation of the values underlying our food culture. Luxury in the world of gastronomy when we started the journey was all about truffles, foie gras, caviar, hand-ironed table clothes, fine dining for the few. We dreamed of redefining luxury. We felt that humble ingredients and a naked table could somehow represent luxury as well. We wanted to emphasize seasonality and restore the link between cooking and nature, and we wanted food to be compatible with healthiness and sustainability.

The second thing we did was to start exploring the idea that if one day our food culture should be counted amongst the most delicious, respected, and admirable in the world, which values should define it? We needed a guiding light for all the stakeholders that we wanted to involve in the project.

What would be the benefits for each of us, for our region, for our industry, and for the planet if we could make it happen? This was how we ended up writing the first draft of the New Nordic Cuisine Manifesto, presented publicly for the first time in 2004 at the New Nordic Cuisine Symposium, after having been debated and reworked by the group of chefs who eventually signed it.

I like to believe that the New Nordic Cuisine was never a declaration of war against French food or Italian pizza, nor a crusade against sushi or Moroccan tagine. That if there is one enemy it is the international junk and fast-food industry dominated by massive corporations that ruin our health, undermine our independence, and potentially damage our planet.

It is common knowledge that we are once more in the middle of a process of mass extinction of the biological species on Earth. This time it is life destroying itself, so to speak, because in a period of about 150 years one very intelligent species seems to be almost single-handedly demolishing its own livelihood as well as large parts of the biosphere.

One billion people are suffering from hunger and poverty and it is incredibly disheartening that another roughly 1.3 billion people at the same time are suffering from obesity. Man holds a unique position amongst the living creatures on Earth, evolution has provided us the ability to think and show compassion. As the spoken word of Leonard Cohen reads, "There is a crack, a crack in everything, that's where the light gets in."

Food matters beyond pleasure. The big idea was to invent a fresher, brighter, juicier cuisine—packed with vegetables and closer to nature. An approach to cooking that would bridge the idea of deliciousness with the health of each individual and of the planet. We hoped to inspire chefs across the globe to create value for the planet as an integral part of their attempt to raise the bar in their restaurants. We hoped that if chefs would stand up to this challenge they would be a source of inspiration to a whole generation outside of the kitchens too. And what's important, wherever we live and whatever we do, is that we once again value the work of farmers, fishermen, foragers, and food producers. That is the only way we truly can return a voice to nature, which is in the interests of us all. In the end, we are all one, and the most important decisions need to be made in the light of eternity.

CLAUS MEYER – *New York City, USA*
Culinary entrepreneur, Agern and The Great Northern Food Hall NYC, co-founder of Meyers and Noma

The aims of the
New Nordic Cuisine Manifesto are:

1   To express the purity, freshness, simplicity, and ethics we wish to associate to our region.

2   To reflect the changes of the seasons in the meals we make.

3   To base our cooking on ingredients and produce whose characteristics are particularly in our climates, landscapes, and waters.

4   To combine the demand for good taste with modern knowledge of health and well-being.

5   To promote Nordic products and the variety of Nordic producers—and to spread the word about their underlying cultures.

6   To promote animal welfare and a sound production process in our seas, on our farmland, and in the wild.

7   To develop potentially new applications of traditional Nordic food products.

8   To combine the best in Nordic cookery and culinary traditions with influences from abroad.

9   To combine local self-suffiency with regional sharing of high-quality products.

10 To join forces with consumer representatives, other cooking craftsmen, agriculture, fishing, food, retail and wholesale industries, researchers, teachers, politicians, and authorities on this project for the benefit and advantage of everyone in the Nordic countries.

GO WILD!
by Roland Rittman

Borderless Co. has asked me to explain how the wild nature of the Nordic countries came to be an inspiration to what is today known as the Nordic kitchen.

It is believed that the 20 years on my knees in the wild, in the business of supplying wild herbs, berries, and mushrooms, has been a conscious strategy to change people's eating habits and their treatment of nature. Although this has come about naturally, as with most things in life, it happened by coincidence.

When I was a child in the city of Trelleborg, Sweden, I would collect insects in the neighboring swamp land. To my misfortune, my place of recreation and solitude in nature was soon turned into the local golf course. The swamp dried up, the plant life, insects, and animals dissipated; the land was claimed, developed, repurposed, and taken away. This experience left an impression that would later shape my greater purpose: to forage and connect with wild nature. If you connect with a piece of nature, area, or parcel of land, you will be willing to fight for it, if there are plans to redevelop it. The strongest connection one can have with nature is to eat from it, to find nutrients and sustenance from its divine creation. Forage, connect, and fight for your nature from impeding urbanization.

My company has worked with restaurants in Denmark, Finland, Norway, The Faroe Islands, and throughout the whole of Sweden, beginning in Scania in 1998. Since then, a conscious awareness of the wild followed the chefs we supply as they spread their food and cooking concepts to other chefs and restaurants.

When I started my company in 2004, the nearby city of Copenhagen had become especially interesting. After having sold to the SAS restaurant Alberto K and several others, I crossed paths with René Redzepi, who was inspired to create a pure Nordic weed kitchen at Noma. Later that year, the meeting was held at which chefs from the Nordic region established the New Nordic Cuisine Manifesto.

My own adventure started when I privately sold wild mushrooms at the market in the city of Lund in 1998 due to a harvest surplus of the mushroom known as *pied bleu* (blue foot). I had in the same city achieved my education in mathematics, chemistry, biology, quaternary geology, and archeology. I opened up a new yet old market by first selling mushrooms and herbs at the market in the morning and, continuing into the afternoon, selling to restaurants in Lund for half the price. This later spanned out to the neighboring cities of Malmö and Helsingborg. When I founded my sole proprietorship, Roland Rittman Jordnära Natur & Kultur, in 2004, and later scaled up my business to my public limited company Roland Rittman AB in 2012, the work continued; now, however, as a full-time occupation, employment, and livelihood.

Almost nobody used my name *jordnära*, Swedish for "living close to the earth," which is also the name of my timber-framed house where it all began. Instead, I had without realizing it, become my own brand, an accredited label highlighted on the menus as "Roland Rittman" while *jordnära* lives on through a customer of mine. Eric Vildgaard adopted the name for his restaurant *jordnära* at the Gentofte Hotel, north of Copenhagen, a restaurant where the wild leaves its mark on the menu.

In the 1960s, as a young amateur field biologist during my teenage years, aware of the threat to the survival of the planet, I was already devoted to actively protecting nature.

We listened to alarm bells of Rachel Carson's *Silent Spring*, and George Borgström, among others, and thought that Armageddon was only a decade away. We acted accordingly and hoped to raise people's awareness. Half a century later, that same crisis is finally accepted as a threat to civilization, and society is starting to become aware and change its behavior. We have a set of genes that allow us to act collectively and selflessly. It is not an attack from outer space we need to worry about: the threat comes from within ourselves and we need to be reprogrammed. It turns out that our eating habits and transitions to an organic and sustainable agriculture, along with reconnecting with nature by eating wild products, will give the power to change—to save the planet and to save ourselves. Now is the time to mobilize all forces. By nature, humankind works best when we interact with one another. An entire generation since the 1980s has been fooled into betting on and investing solely in themselves. From 1975 onwards, the Barsebäck Nuclear Power Plant, located in the middle of Örestad, threatened the millions of people around it until its closure in 2005. The two reactors were situated 20 kilometers from the center of Copenhagen—the capital of Denmark! I became aware of the problem in 1973 and acted accordingly. On my initiative, the first Nordic Barsebäck march was organized in 1976 and the marches continued until 1986 (the year of the Chernobyl disaster). They peaked in 1977 with 20,000–30,000 people protesting in front of the nuclear power plant. Two serious accidents in Barsebäck could have led to a Nordic Fukushima!

I raised my voice about many local environmental issues. Since then, my concern has grown from local to regional to widespread Nordic issues, especially the merging of Zealand and Scania, the Örestad project. The bridge between Sweden and Denmark was central to the attempt to move the population to a few major centers. The establishment continues in its efforts to urbanize people around the globe. But it is not too late to leave behind consumerism in the metropolitan areas and follow the strong green wave and global search for sustainable solutions.

Considering my significant involvement, I can describe myself as an energetic strategist and one of the pioneers of the Swedish environmental debate since 1963. Today I direct my energy toward foraging and the supply of wild products to restaurants in the Nordic countries, especially those of Copenhagen, which I visit twice a week. For a few years, I had a couple of employees and managed the company from an agricultural property and farm without the aid of cultivated land. This proved difficult to sustain as chefs adopted my concept, acquired their own knowledge and developed an interest in foraging themselves. It paved the way, however, for positive outcomes, as the ideas of foraging for wild food spread more widely and rapidly.

Now at the age of 71, I have no plans to retire because there is a certain thrill in being part of the Nordic Kitchen, and an excitement in seeing where and how far it will go. It is a gastronomic cosmos in which we foragers and suppliers, together with restaurants, chefs, and culinary entrepreneurs, orbit around the center. Now gastro-tourists flock to the Nordic countries to eat at gourmet restaurants, and choose them as an alternative to Paris, Rome, and Barcelona. We can only expect exponential growth in the region's food culture to live up to the expectations of the outside world.

We in the Nordic countries have put a world at our feet by falling on our knees for the richness and abundance of nature. The concept is spreading globally at the speed of thought, illuminating minds and helping us to stay human. We go wild to rescue humanity and the planet with it.

The Noma team have taken this idea to heart, commencing a global campaign for wild food through their app VILD MAD, dedicated to the edible wild landscape. The ambition, is to implement these teachings throughout the world, to educate young people with a skill as valuable and important as the skill of reading and writing.

The wild revolution did not start in the Nordic countries, however. The gathering heritage of indigenous people has survived, scattered across the world. A forgotten wisdom to be relearned, a renaissance of the original foods. One of the most beautiful results of this culinary revolution is that indigenous people are restoring their dignity, as their knowledge is recognized once again as important for our common future.

This gastronomic, culinary, cultural, global, and revolutionary movement needs a rite of passage, an initiation ceremony—some ritual event that marks a person's transition from one status to another.

- Go to the beach or to the woods or to some part of nature that you have made your own
- Kneel on the ground
- Humbly bend your head
- Take a bite from a rooted plant
- Graze like the animal you are
- Contemplate with universal empathy our critical impact on this wild symphony of existence
- Thank the sun for giving us energy, green plants, animals, and life
- Infuse your identity with the Earth
- Join the revolution
- GO WILD!

ROLAND RITTMAN – *Anderslöv, Sweden*
Forager and Environmental Activist

Ulo – Hotel Arctic | Ilulissat, Greenland, Denmark

Overlooking the awe-inspiring floating glaciers of the Ilulissat Icefjord and igloos spanning the neighboring cliffs that descend into the deep blue of the bone-numbing Arctic Ocean, restaurant Ulo honors regional culinary traditions with its contemporary, complex, and often daring set menu under head chef Heine Rynkeby Knudsen.

Heine Rynkeby Knudsen

— Head chef

My adventure in Greenland started in spring 2016, after a little research from home. At the time, I did not know what I had agreed to, but I was quickly and pleasantly surprised. Never had I worked somewhere both so remote and so incredibly dynamic. Most of the inhabitants here are self-sufficient. Fishing is the main source of income in the city, so we can always be sure to get the freshest catch. When we fillet our fish, they are still skidding and flailing. It is an honor to work with such fresh and local raw materials—an environment I urge any chef to experience.

Our dishes are simple and focus solely on the Greenlandic. Aside from fresh fish, reindeer, and muskox (depending on the hunting season), our menu also features mollusks, crustaceans, and locally picked herbs.

I work with one of the wildest kitchens in the world. It is an engagement that requires a progressive vision along with the honorable opportunity to influence how the world interprets Greenlandic cuisine. With the honor comes a huge responsibility, and a task that I embrace with great humility and respect.

Ulo – Hotel Arctic – Ilulissat, Greenland, Denmark

Arctic char, Arctic white heather, blue mussels, and angelica

Preparation

Serves 4

ARCTIC CHAR

400 g / 14 oz Arctic char
1 1/2 pt water
10 g / 2 tsp salt

Blend the water with the salt until it dissolves. Place the Arctic char in the saltwater for 10 minutes. Remove the fish and dry it in a kitchen towel to remove excess liquid.

PICKLED ANGELICA

200 ml / ¾ cup water
200 g / 7 oz sugar
200 ml / ¾ cup organic apple cider vinegar
1 bay leaf
½ shallot
5 peppercorns
1 angelica stem

Boil the water, sugar, vinegar, bay leaf, shallot, and peppercorns. Remove the pickle from heat and allow to infuse for 10 minutes. Cut the angelica into slices and place in the warm pickle. Pour the pickled angelica into a preserving jar rinsed with Atamon (sodium benzoate). Place the jar in a pantry for approximately 1 month.

FERMENTED GLASSWORT

20 glasswort
2% salt brine

Thoroughly wash the glasswort and place in a vacuum bag together with a 2% salt brine. Place the vacuum-sealed glasswort in a pantry and check daily to see if gases have expanded in the vacuum bag. Release the gases from the bag, then seal again. Let the glasswort ferment for approximately 3 months.

MUSSEL BOUILLON/ CONSOMMÉ

1 kg / 2 lb 3 oz blue mussels
1 carrot
2 stems celery
1 large onion
300 ml / 1⅓ cups seawater from the Ilulissat Icefjord
8 stems thyme
2 tsp egg whites
1 lemon

Clean and debeard the mussels thoroughly.

Chop the carrot, celery, and onion into small cubes and sauté in a little oil with the thyme. Then put the cleaned mussels and seawater into a new pot and steam, covered with a lid. Strain the liquid. Blend the egg whites with the mussels. Now, stir the mussel and egg white mixture into the vegetable soup and slowly bring to a boil.

The egg whites retain the impurities and the mussels help to preserve the taste. Gently strain the soup through a cloth to achieve a clear liquid. Season with lemon juice.

PLATING
Arctic white heather

Bake the Arctic char on a kettle grill for 2–3 minutes with a lot of heather to hot smoke the fish. The Arctic char may be a little raw in the center when serving. Remove the skin from the Arctic char and arrange the fermented glasswort, pickled angelica, and mountain flowers on top of the fish. Pour the mussel bouillon at the table.

About the Dish

Arctic char is one of the best fish I have eaten here. Since the season is short and the Arctic char must be used as quickly as possible, however I have become increasingly inspired by the traditional method of smoking fish.

Arctic char is traditionally caught by hand in the river. The fish is then salted and smoked with all the bountiful flora the mountain has to offer: Arctic white heather, Labrador tea, blackberry, and juniper berry. All these flavors penetrate the flesh of the fish. We hot smoke the Arctic char on the grill with heather and serve the dish with a mussel bouillon, pickled angelica, fermented glasswort, and mountain flowers.

I have, with the exception of one element, taken all that Greenland has to offer. The Arctic char lives in the same place as the mussels in the bays where they spawn; the angelica grows near the same streams and rivers that the Arctic char swim up; in Greenland, fish are traditionally smoked with heather. This is one of the dishes that I really believe captures the essence and taste of Greenland.

Qajaasat with white chocolate and gooseberries

Preparation

CRYSTALLIZED WHITE
CHOCOLATE

**100 ml / just under
½ cup water
200 g / 7 oz sugar
150 g / 5.5 oz white
chocolate
1 tbsp dried harebell
1 tbsp dried chamomile
1 tbsp dried blueberries**

Boil the water with the sugar at
145°C (295°F). In the meantime,
melt the white chocolate. When
the sugar brine reaches 145°C
(295°F), whip it in the white
chocolate to make the mixture
grainy and crispy.

Grind the dried harebell,
dried chamomile, and dried
blueberries with a coffee
grinder until fine powder.
Mix with the crystallized
white chocolate.

GOOSEBERRY PUREE

**300 g / 10.5 oz
gooseberries
handful of sugar
lemon juice**

Boil the gooseberries and sugar
until color turns reddish. Season
with a little lemon juice. Blend
to a smooth a puree. Strain and
put in a piping pastry bag.

WHITE CHOCOLATE/
ARCTIC LABRADOR TEA
PARFAIT

**8 g / ½ tbsp Arctic
Labrador tea (*qajaasat*)
500 ml / 2¼ cup cream**

Make a cream of Arctic
Labrador tea, by boiling the
cream with the tea leaves.
Let the cream sit overnight.
Strain it the next day.

**300 g / 10.5 oz Arctic
Labrador tea cream
100 g / 3.5 oz sugar
200 g / 7 oz white
chocolate
160 g / 5.5 oz
powdered sugar
200 g / 7 oz egg yolk
700 g / 1 lb 9 oz cream
200 g / 7 oz white
chocolate (for dipping)**

Boil the Arctic Labrador
tea cream with sugar, and pour
it over the white chocolate.
Make sure the cream is not too
hot when you pour it over the
chocolate to avoid the chocolate
to coagulate. Stir the mass
until the chocolate is dissolved.
Let the mixture slowly cool to
room temperature.

Whip the egg yolk and powdered sugar into an airy eggnog
and stir it together with the
Arctic Labrador Tea/chocolate
mixture. Whip 700 g (1 lb 9 oz)
of cream and stir into the rest.
Pour the parfait into half sphere
molds and place in the freezer.
When frozen, connect into
spheres. Dip them in 200 g (7 oz)
melted white chocolate mixed
with a little of the powder of
berries and pollen from the
dried harebell, dried chamomile,
and dried blueberry. Store the
parfait spheres in the freezer
until serving.

PLATING
**Arctic Labrador tea
branches**

Place 1 tbsp of the gooseberry
puree in the bottom part of
the plate and sprinkle 1 tbsp of
the crystallized white chocolate/
pollen over half of the
gooseberry puree. Serve the
parfait on a separate plate
on top of branches of the
Arctic Labrador tea. Arrange
the parfait on top of the
gooseberry puree.

About the Dish

This dish is inspired by two things:
the herb *qajaasat* (Grønlandspost
or Arctic Labrador tea), which is
used mostly for tea and smoking
fish, and the Greenlandic cairns
that surround the mountains. You
could say that this dish started with
these aesthetics and developed into
a soft, sour, and spicy dessert.

The Arctic Labrador tea is
prepared a bit like tea, but rather
than being steeped in water, it
is cooked in cream to transfer the
flavor to it. The cream is then
used for a white chocolate parfait,
which we serve with gooseberry
puree and crystallized white
chocolate sprinkled with pollen
from dried flowers and berries.

Whale, juniper berries, and mountain sorrel

Preparation

Serves 4

WHALE TARTARE

350 g / 12 oz narwhal
2 beets
1 lemon, zested and
juiced
salt, to taste

To make the tartare, scrape the meat with a sharp knife. Then mix with grated lemon zest, lemon juice, and salt.

Boil the beets in lightly salted water and peel when they are tender. Place the beets in a dehydrator and let them dry for approximately 24 hours, depending on their size. The beets must be completely dry before they are grated.

JUNIPER GEL

200 ml / ¾ cup water
200 g / 7 oz sugar
200 ml / ¾ cup organic
apple cider vinegar
8 fresh juniper berries
4 juniper branches
5 g / 1 tsp Gellan

Boil the water, sugar and apple cider vinegar to make a pickle. Add fresh juniper berries and juniper branches and let the pickle sit for 1 week.

Strain the pickle. Then boil, add the Gellan and blend into the pickle. Bring the pickle to a boil again, but only for 30 seconds.

Refrigerate the pickle overnight, so that it becomes a firm gelatin. Then blend it into a smooth cream. Put it in a pastry bag.

PLATING

cress
mountain sorrel

Shape the whale tartare into a circle with a round cutter. Layer small bits of juniper gel on top of the whale. Cover the tartare with a mixture of mountain sorrel and cress. Grate the dehydrated beet over the tartare—but not too much, otherwise the dish will become too sweet.

About the Dish

The whale is a majestic animal that deserves respect in every way, and consuming it is a very controversial subject all over the world.

In Greenland, we live in an isolated Arctic climate with access to a very limited range of foods. For many generations, whale has been an indispensable source of nutrition. A single whale can feed a whole village for a long period of time, which is vital to survival. In addition to the whale meat, all other parts of the whale are used. The fat is used for making candles and the baleen plates for clothes and jewelry. Whales are incredibly nutritious and have been the means of survival in the countryside during the very cold and isolated winter months. Although it is a simple tartare, it is a unique taste experience, bringing together five ingredients: whale meat with juniper berry gel, dried beet, cress, and mountain sorrel.

PONY | Copenhagen, Zealand, Denmark

Lighthearted, casual dining with no sacrifice of quality, where chef Lars Lundø Jakobsen takes his diners on a ride through the seasons. Part of the Kadeau family, the name PONY alludes to the past of the neighboring Sorte Hest—or Black Horse—where the weary farmers from the Vesterbro guesthouse would eat on their commute to the business districts of Copenhagen.

Lars Lundø Jakobsen

– Head chef

Charm, reliability, and quality form the foundations of a popular new category in the gastronomy industry: so-called little-sister restaurants, which have started to pop up all over the city. Enter PONY—a simple place to eat without compromising on quality.

Since opening in 2012, PONY has been a frontrunner of gastronomy in Copenhagen's mid-market. Its success is based on its desire to be a restaurant of high standard, operating with the same values and love of quality ingredients as the acclaimed, established Nordic restaurants of Denmark, serving inventive contemporary dishes made from seasonal, locally sourced ingredients in a casual setting. The restaurant was founded on the owners' love of running a restaurant in Vesterbro—the place where Kadeau restaurant was founded and where the owners and their families reside.

Served in a relaxing setting, the menu is composed of seasonal, local, and organic ingredients; animal welfare is a priority whenever meat and fish are served. The dishes may seem simple at first glance, like something you could make at home, but deep flavor and finesse set them apart from home cooking. The wine list is put together based on the same principles of class and excellence, featuring wines made by people who seek quality over quantity.

PONY bread

Preparation

1 loaf yields 12 slices

DOUGH

- 18 g / 0.6 oz yeast
- 100 g / just under ½ cup natural yogurt
- 125 g / ½ cup dark beer
- 500 ml / 1 pt water
- 55 g / 1 cup coarse oatmeal
- 625 g / 1 lb 6 oz wheat flour
- 30 g / 2 tbsp salt

DAY 1:

Mix together all the ingredients in a large bowl, cover the bowl, and refrigerate to cool-rise overnight.

DAY 2:

Remove the bowl from refrigerator and let the dough rise at room temperature for 3–4 hours or until it has doubled in size. Then, heat an enameled cast iron pot to 250°C (480°F).

Scrape the dough into the pot and bake for 45 minutes with the lid on, and then another 20–25 minutes with the lid off. Let the bread cool on a wire rack for 30 minutes.

BUTTER

- 250 g / 9 oz butter
- 50 g / ¼ cup buttermilk

Whisk room-temperature butter until white and airy using an electric whisk. At lower speed, stir in the buttermilk and whisk until homogeneous.

PLATING

Break the bread into smaller pieces and toast for 5–6 minutes at 200°C (390°F). Serve immediately with the butter. The butter can be stored in the refrigerator for 4–5 days. It just needs to be tempered and whisked again.

About the Dish

The PONY bread has been with us and Kadeau since the beginning—and will undoubtedly be served until our last day. It is a bread that does not require large machinery or technical skills—just good ingredients and time. It is served warm with a hearty smear of whipped butter. We consider it maximum pleasure with minimal effort!

Braised pork chest, grilled leeks, mustard gravy, and pork crackling

Preparation

Serves 4

DAY 1:

BRAISED PORK CHEST

**800 g / 1 lb 12 oz pork
chest with bones and
crackling
salt
pepper
lemon thyme
400 g / 14 oz celeriac,
carrot, onion, and
garlic (soup vegetables)
200 g / ⅞ cup chicken stock**

Remove the bones from the pork and cut off the crackling as one piece. Season the meat with salt, pepper, and lemon thyme. Place in a casserole dish onto the previously removed bones, minced soup vegetables, and chicken stock. Cover with aluminum foil and roast for 10–12 hours at 75°C (165°F). Let the meat cool under pressure until the next day and strain the pork stock (approximately 250 g / 8.8 oz) for the sauce.

Cut the crackling into 5 mm (0.2 in) wide strips and boil until tender in salted water. Drain and spread out on a silicone baking mat. Dry in the oven while the meat cooks for 10–12 hours or until completely dry.

LEEK OIL

12 mini leeks

**200 ml / ⅞ cup
grapeseed oil**

Cut off the bottoms and tops of the leeks and save the stems for the next day. Clean the tops and toast in the oven at 130°C (265°F) for 45 minutes or until golden and dry. Blend with the grapeseed oil for 10 minutes. Strain the oil and store in the refrigerator for the emulsion.

DAY 2:

Deep-fry the dried crackling strips in oil at 180°C (365°F) until they are puffy and crispy. Place on fat-absorbing paper and sprinkle them with salt. Break into smaller pieces.

MUSTARD GRAVY

**80 g / 3 oz egg whites
8 g / 1⅓ tsp salt
15 ml / 1 tbsp apple
 cider vinegar
50 g / ¼ cup butter
20 g / 1½ tbsp wheat flour
2 tbsp coarse mustard
30 g / 2 tbsp nasturtiums
 (both leaves and flowers)
50 g / 2 oz pickled leek
 flowers (flowers from
 chives can also be used)
apple cider vinegar,
 to taste
pork stock**

Mix the egg whites, leek oil, salt, and apple cider vinegar in a tall container. Emulsify with a powerful hand blender and adjust the thickness with a bit of cold water until creamy. Add salt and apple cider vinegar to taste.

Brown the butter in a small sauce pan. Add the wheat flour and whisk to form a roux. Add pork stock bit by bit while stirring. Boil the gravy and add mustard, salt, and apple cider vinegar to taste. Pluck, rinse, and spin the nasturtiums in a salad spinner. Pluck the pickled leek flowers from the stems.

PLATING

Cut the meat into four elongated slices. Brown on a hot skillet and warm in oven for 5–6 minutes at 200°C (390°F). On the same hot skillet, grill the leeks in the pork fat until tender and toasted. Add salt and pepper to taste. Then, warm the gravy and add salt, pepper, and mustard to taste. Place 1 tbsp of leek emulsion on one side of the plate. The other side should be arranged in the following order: the meat, grilled leeks, pickled leek flowers. Garnish with 3–4 tbsp of mustard gravy, some pork crackling, and nasturtiums.

About the Dish

This dish is a perfect example of something that might look simple but that, in reality, involves precise technical skills, maximizes the utility of all the ingredients, and has a special depth of flavor. You can always make a pot roast and some roasted root vegetables— but the satisfaction of preparing gravy from scratch with puffy crackling and pickled leek blossoms in summer is hard to beat.

Kadeau | Copenhagen, Zealand, Denmark

Memories of an alpine ski lodge are reawakened, and timber and textured wood strengthen this connection. The axe fixed in the stump, a remnant of the log splitting needed to fuel the fire of the smoke house. The warm glow of the flames radiates from the open-plan copper kitchen to meet the dining room floor, where the nature of Bornholm is plated as a *bornholmerbank*.

Nicolai Nørregaard

– Head chef & co-founder

The story of Kadeau is rooted in ambitions and youthful gumption that, over time, developed to become a part of the established elite of Danish gastronomy. What started out as a three-course menu in a repurposed beach hut with an ice cream parlor in the back has evolved into 20-course dinners today. The restaurant's ambition was—and still is—to use resources unique to Bornholm that will delight our guests. We pick, gather, and harvest from our own garden and the wild; we also collaborate with farmers in Bornholm as well as raw material suppliers country wide.

Our courses are expressive but focused. They can entail many flavors yet always balance in taste. Over time we have continued to push the boundaries and challenge both our guests and ourselves. However, we are always mindful that this should not happen at the expense of the meal's overall balance.

The Kadeau kitchen is characterized by the huge amount of ingredients we pickle each year. Whether celery, pinecones, herbs, or berries, we harvest them when they are in season and pickle, salt, or ferment them. By doing so, our kitchen can use a variety of products throughout the long and barren winter. Pickling and fermenting is not only a matter of flavor, it is a gastronomical tradition of Denmark, which has become intertwined with our expression and image.

Celeriac, woodruff, ants, caviar, and fermented white asparagus

Preparation

Serves 4

WOODRUFF OIL

20 g / 4 tsp fresh woodruff
neutral oil

Blend oil and woodruff at highest speed for 2 minutes. Then strain the pulp through a cloth.

GEL PICKLE

500 g / 1 pt vinegar
250 ml / 1⅛ cup water
175 g / 6 oz sugar
6 g / 1 tsp Gellan
6 g / 1 tsp Citras

Mix vinegar, water, and sugar with Citras and Gellan. Bring to a boil and blend with a hand mixer. Once cool, blend until completely smooth with a blender and finish it off with a little bit of woodruff oil.

HAY ASH
hay

Burn a handful of hay. When cooled, pass through a sieve, and use the ash.

HAY-BAKED CELERIAC

1 head celeriac
neutral oil
salt
hay

Clean the celeriac thoroughly. Then rub it in oil and salt. Bake in hay until completely tender at approximately 2 hours at 170°C (340°F). Cut into 2 cm (0.8 in) thin slices. Finally, cut these slices into round shapes using a round cutter.

FERMENTED ASPARAGUS SAUCE

100 g / 3.5 oz butter
100 g / ⅓ cup fermented
  asparagus juice
a pinch of xanthan gum
50 g / 3½ tbsp buttermilk
apple cider vinegar
salt

Heat the butter and fermented asparagus juice. Mix with a pinch of xanthan gum and then with buttermilk. Adjust the taste with salt and apple cider vinegar.

PLATING

60 wood ants
50 g / 1.7 oz Osetra caviar

Toast a piece of the celeriac in butter until golden brown. Dab off the fat and brush with gel pickle. Then sprinkle about 15 ants over the celeriac's surface, followed by a bit of hay ash on top. Arrange the caviar around the celeriac and add 2 tbsp of warm fermented asparagus sauce.

About the Dish

This is a dish that pulls strongly in many directions, but is bound together by an intense taste experience. Celeriac is a vegetable that can provide the most intense flavors. The flavor is drawn out with the smoke from the fireplace. The depth and width comes from the caviar and fermented white asparagus and buttermilk. It is in many ways a very Kadeau-esque dish, with deep and broad flavor, balanced with the fresh acid from Bornholm wood ants. We are proud to use a vegetable that so far, we've only dreamed of sourcing from Bornholm: the stunning white asparagus from farmer Søren Wiuff.

"What's-in-the-garden-right-now" tartlet

Preparation

Serves 4

CEP TART CRUST

**150 g / 5 oz "Ølands"
wheat flour (or spelt)
3 g / a pinch of salt
4 g / a pinch of cep
mushroom powder**
(*Boletus edulis*)
25 ml / 5 tsp water

Mix the dry ingredients: flour,
salt, and cep mushroom powder.
Add water and stir into a dough.
Refrigerate for 1 hour. Then,
roll out the dough thinly and
bake in tart shell molds at 150°C
(300°F) until golden brown.

CHERRY BLOSSOM OIL

**100 g / ⅓ cup oil
20 g / 4 tsp cherry
blossoms**

Blend the oil and cherry
blossoms for 2 minutes and
drain the pulp through a cloth.

REDUCED BUTTERMILK
WHEY
1 1 / 2 pt buttermilk

Warm up the buttermilk until
it curdles. Then, reduce
the whey to 50 g (1.7 oz).

KING CRAB
**100 g / 3.5 oz king crab
butter**

Pick the meat from the king
crab shell and fry in butter.
Finely chop.

CARAMELIZED CREAM
200 g / 7 oz organic cream

Warm a nonstick saucepan
until hot. Add the cream and
let it reduce to almost nothing.
Then, use a spatula to loosen
the brown, caramelized cream.
Finally, whip the cream until
homogenous with a whisk.

FRIED CABBAGE
AND GARLIC

**200 g / 7 oz mixed
cabbage shoots
4 garlic cloves with roots**

Wash the cabbage and garlic.
Cut the roots from the garlic
bulbs. Fry the cabbage and
garlic until crisp and golden.
Chop everything finely and
season with salt.

PLATING

Mix the fried king crab meat
with caramelized cream.
Season with salt and fill the
cep tart crust. Drip 5 drops
of cherry blossom oil and 5
drops of reduced buttermilk
whey on top of the crab
mixture. Assemble a mountain
of fried cabbage and garlic
on top, and serve.

About the Dish

There is something beautiful—also
a little provocative—in serving
a meal that consists of one bite.
We enjoy, however, varying the
size of the servings throughout
the course. In this little tartlet, we
present the majestic king crab that
lives in colder climates than that
of the island of Bornholm. The
dish is complete when topped with
the vegetables we currently have
to hand in our own garden. This
beautiful bite often changes its
appearance depending on what
our garden in Bornholm has to
offer and proves our deep loyalty
to the produce of the island, while
not being prevented from sourcing
the best raw materials elsewhere.

Ember-baked kohlrabi, black-current leaves, and rhubarb root

Preparation

Serves 4

EMBER-BAKED KOHLRABI
2 heads kohlrabi

Place the kohlrabi in hot embers, covering them. It takes about 15 minutes for the kohlrabi to get a crispy shell and to become easy to prepare. Then let cool. When cold enough, peel off the outer shell and scoop into balls using a Parisienne scoop.

RHUBARB ROOT OIL

20 g / 4 tsp rhubarb root, rinsed and cleaned
100 g / ⅓ cup neutral oil

Blend the rinsed rhubarb root with oil for 2 minutes. Strain the pulp through a cloth.

BLACKCURRANT OIL

20 g / 4 tsp fresh blackcurrant leaves
100 g / ⅓ cup neutral oil

Blend the blackcurrant leaves with oil for 2 minutes. Strain the pulp through a cloth.

FIR "CRUMBLE"

pickled nobilis fir
pickled blackcurrant leaves
pickled Norway spruce

Take equal parts of pickled nobilis fir, pickled blackcurrant leaves, and pickled Norway spruce and chop finely.

WHITE CURRANT SAUCE

50 g / 10 tsp white currant juice
fermented pea juice
salt

Flavor the white currant juice with a small amount of fermented pea juice and some salt.

NOBILIS FIR CONES
pickled nobilis fir cones

Cut the pickled nobilis cones into thin sticks.

SPINACH PUREE
200 g / 7 oz baby spinach

Wash the baby spinach and cook in a saucepan with a splash of water for 2–3 minutes or until the spinach has wilted. Cool slightly, then blend to a smooth puree. Add some water if needed.

PLATING

Marinate the kohlrabi balls in some spinach puree. Add salt and rhubarb root oil to taste. Then place the chopped pickles on top of each piece of kohlrabi. Afterwards add a single piece of nobilis fir. Mix the white currant sauce with a little blackcurrant and rhubarb root oil and serve.

ICE BOWL

Place ice cubes over the bottom of a bowl and center a glass on top of the ice cubes. Weigh down the glass with more ice cubes. Use freezer tape to fix the glass in its position. Pour cold water between bowl and glass and place in the freezer. When frozen, remove the tape and ice cubes from glass. Fill the glass with warm, not hot water and let stand for 1–2 minutes. Gently lift glass out of the bowl. Then dip the bowl into warm water and remove from the ice bowl.

About the Dish

This dish combines both the old and new of Kadeau by way of an ordinary vegetable. Long before we began to grow kohlrabi, it was extensively used in Danish restaurants, though usually only in its raw form. At Kadeau, we heat and smoke the kohlrabi inside a fireplace, which turns the vegetable into a new, playful element of our menu. This dish would not be complete, however, without adding homemade and self-pickled produce from Bornholm and giving it a touch of fire. This method not only deepens the flavor of the dish but also enhances its freshness, acidity, and aroma. Bornholm's pickling bar is present in the marinade of blackcurrant oil and rhubarb root, in the sauce of white currant and fermented pea juice, and in the pickled spruce and pickled blackcurrant leaves sprinkled on top of it. It is complete when served in an iced bowl.

Hotel Frederiksminde | Præstø, Zealand, Denmark

The historically restored eighteenth-century Hotel Frederiksminde, with panoramic views of Præstø Fjord and an intriguing eclectic array of décor, is home to the kitchen of chef Jonas Mikkelsen. Here, simplicity is key and the finest seasonal produce procured from the water's edge or the neighboring woodlands form the foundation of the menu.

Jonas Mikkelsen

— Head chef & partner

We are beholden to the seasons and to the gems of the forest, and we take it upon ourselves to forage wild herbs, mushrooms, and vegetables. We serve our wild finds immediately, or preserve our gatherings through drying and fermentation techniques for the bleak winter months. Nature can be seen throughout all our dishes. It's the key influence and point of reference in the way we envisage and prepare our dishes. It was when I started at Frederiksminde and began to work in a place surrounded by nature, that I truly discovered my voice as a chef and the type of food that is closest to my heart.

A culinary experience at Frederiksminde is achieved only through the finest raw materials, some of which we have planted and grown in our own soil, others we have gathered in nature. The meat and poultry are procured through local boutique farms. It is not a priority for us to have a specific national Danish or regional Nordic signature, as long as we are local and cook with flavor, love, and honesty. From farm to fork. We see to the garden and reap the soil ourselves. Chefs and apprentices alike have carefully planted each and every seed and cutting, some with great results and others that prove a little harder to propagate. We are constantly learning, and enjoy seeing our farm thrive. Our kitchen garden has grown year on year and the number of vegetables from our own production has multiplied. During the seasons of spring and summer, the vegetables harvested in the morning are then plated in the evening.

Hotel Frederiksminde – Præstø, Zealand, Denmark

Salted mackerel with sour cream, pickled green tomatoes, and mustard salad

Preparation

Serves 4

SALTED MACKEREL

**4 fillets of mackerel
salt
sugar**

Salt the mackerel and sprinkle with sugar. Let it sit for 24 hours. Freeze, take out, then prepare.

SOUR CREAM

**200 ml / 1 cup organic cream
juice from ½ a lemon
salt**

Lightly whip the cream and refrigerate for 2 hours. Add lemon and salt to taste.

WALNUTS
4 walnuts

Blanch, then peel off the skin.

GREEN TOMATOES

**2 small green tomatoes
water
sugar
vinegar**

Buy in season. Poke a hole with a skewer and pickle in a brine made from equal parts water, sugar, and vinegar.

MUSTARD SALAD

Pluck and clean.

PLATING

Place the mackerel on the plate. Then place the pickled tomato, walnuts, and salad next to it. Serve the sour cream separately.

About the Dish

Danish mackerel is probably one of my favorite fish due to its rich fattiness and the way it almost melts in your mouth when served raw—which is why we serve it this way. We combine it with sour cream to balance out the fatty mackerel, while the sweet-and-sour, pickled green tomatoes add freshness to this dish. The bitterness of the walnuts and the mustard salad round off the taste experience.

Pumpkin ice cream with a soup of fermented honey, whey, and sea roses

Preparation

Serves 4

PUMPKIN ICE CREAM

1.5 g / a pinch of Cremodan
2 sheets of gelatin
600 g / 1lb 5 oz pumpkin puree
300 g / 10.5 oz brine (equal parts sugar/water and a bit of lemon juice)

Boil the brine with Cremodan. Add the softened gelatin. Mix with the pumpkin puree and some lemon juice. Pour into Pacojet containers.

FERMENTED HONEY

honey
water

It takes about 2–3 months to make. Boiling water is poured over the honey and stored in Mason jars. Once in a while, open the lid to release the pressure. Let sit for 2–3 months at room temperature.

WHEY
1 1/2 pt buttermilk

Pour the buttermilk into a coffee filter and strain the whey from the milk. Let sit for 24 hours.

PICKLED SEA ROSES

sea roses
sugar
water

Gather when in season. Pickle in equal parts sugar and water.

SOUP

whey
fermented honey

Add ⅔ of the whey and ⅓ fermented honey, as well as brine from the sea roses, depending on the sweetness you'd like the soup to have.

YOGURT SNOW

350 ml / 1⅓ cups + ¼ cup water
70 g / 2.5 oz sugar
500 ml / 2¼ cups sheep's milk yogurt
10 g / a squeeze of lemon juice

Heat the water, sugar, and lemon juice together. Let it cool and mix with the yogurt. Freeze in a container and grate with a fork while frozen.

PLATING

Use an ice-cold plate so it does not melt straight away. Place the yogurt snow on the bottom, then put a quenelle of pumpkin ice on top of it and one sea rose petal on top of that. Serve the soup separately.

About the Dish

This very simple dessert is inspired by our surroundings, especially the sea roses from the beach just 50 meters away from the hotel, as well as the local summer honey. It really tastes like summer—and is supposed to make you feel that way too!

Høst & Vækst | Copenhagen, Zealand, Denmark

Høst and Vækst—two restaurants—are each other's inverse, yet they are interconnected, carving out a natural ecosystem. One is a symbol of blooming—*vækst* is the Danish word for "growth"—sprouting and prosperity, while the other is a symbol of what naturally follows, a harvest—*høst* is the Danish word for "harvest." Together, Høst and Vækst are passionate interpretations of the contemporary Nordic kitchen.

Jonas Christensen

– Head chef (left), Høst & Vækst

Anders Rytter

– Assistant head chef, Høst

Refuse, reuse. Granite, polished concrete, wood, zinc, and brick: Høst's interior (pictured right), built from reclaimed materials, is a testament to contemporary Nordic design. A space of balanced simplicity that heightens the senses, an awarded design collaboration by Copenhagen's Norm Architects and Danish designers Menu. Then there is the food! Høst has fine-tuned a menu traditionally reserved for boutique establishments to deliver a consistent offering to 200+ covers a night.

At Vækst, the symbol of "growth" is evident upon arrival in the restaurant situated on Sankt Peders Stræde. Nature has been brought indoors, as guests dine in the garden of a two-story greenhouse created using recycled materials by Danish design studio Genbyg. Large glass facades, natural light, raw granite stone walls, wooden furnishings, and plants create the setting for an evening at Vækst.

Grilled beef tenderloin

About the Dish

In theory, as soon as you put a puree and soft onions on top of a piece of beef, you get the classic taste of Danish *hakkebøf*.

The smoked goat cheese grated on top of the mountain of cress covering the beef adds a particular barbeque flavor. By playing on the simple ingredients and minimalist design, the idea of this dish, served at Høst, was to reinvent the classic staple crofting dish, Danish *hakkebøf* with soft onions and sauce.

Preparation

Serves 4

TENDERLOIN

600 g / 1 lb 5 oz beef tenderloin from Grambogård

Suspend the tenderloin on a hook inside the refrigerator for 2 days. Separate meat from ligaments and fat. Wrap the meat and store it in the refrigerator for 5 days. Flip it once per day. After 5 days, remove it from the refrigerator 2 hours before the intended time of cooking. Then, grill it in 4–5 intervals of 5–8 minutes. This should take about 45 minutes with an additional 20 minutes of resting. Slice into 130 g (4.5 oz) portions just before serving.

CARAMELIZED ONION PUREE

500 g / 1 lb 5 oz yellow onions
oil
50 g / 10 tsp apple cider vinegar
2 cloves garlic
50 g / ¼ cup butter

Peel and coarsely chop the onions. Brown them in oil. Let the liquid reduce and then pour over the vinegar. Let that reduce until it has almost evaporated; then add the butter. Let it boil until dark brown. Blend until it resembles a smooth puree.

PICKLED GHERKINS

200 g / 7 oz gherkins
salt
50 g / 10 tsp apple cider vinegar
50 ml / ¼ cup water
1 g / a pinch of fennel
1 g / a pinch of peppercorns

Buy gherkins in season and peel them. Salt for 5 hours and then rinse. Boil everything except for the gherkins. Let cool. Vacuum-pack the gherkins together with the mixture and let it pickle for at least 2 weeks before use. Cut into cubes on the day of use.

SMOKED CHEESE

100 g / 3.5 oz goat cream cheese
5 g / 1 tsp beech wood dust

Smoke the cheese over the beech wood dust while wrapped in cling wrap. Let it sit for 30 minutes. Afterwards, roll 3 cylinders with a diameter of 4 cm (1.5 in) and put them into a freezer. Remove the cling wrap and grate before serving.

PLATING
20 g / 0.7 oz cress

Arrange the tenderloin with a spoonful of onion puree, pickled gherkins, and cress, and grate the frozen smoked cheese over the top. Place the meat on a warm plate.

Grilled Norway lobster with pickled carrots, preserved cornflowers, and elderflowers

Preparation

Serves 4

DRIED CORNFLOWER AND CHAMOMILE

Pluck the petals off all the corn- and chamomile flowers you can get your hands on during the season. Dry them overnight in a dehydrator.

CHAMOMILE PICKLED CARROTS

600 g / 2½ cups vinegar
40 g / 8 tsp chamomile flowers
500 ml / 1 pt water
500 g / 1 lb sugar
400 g / 14 oz carrots

Vacuum-pack the vinegar and chamomile flowers at least 2 months before the intended date of serving. Then, bring the water and sugar to a boil. Pour in the chamomile vinegar and let the mixture cool down. Now, peel the carrots and grate them into threads on a Japanese mandolin. Vacuum-pack the carrots together with the mixture. Place it in the refrigerator for at least 2 days.

NORWAY LOBSTER

8 Norway lobsters (langoustines) –
1 kg / 2 lb 3 oz grapeseed oil, for brushing

Remove the lobster tails and use the shell and heads for the browned lobster butter. Brush the tails lightly with oil and grill them on their red side until they are about room temperature underneath. Place on a plate and let everything breathe.

BROWNED NORWAY LOBSTER BUTTER

8 Norway lobster shells and heads
250 g / 1⅛ cups butter
1 clove garlic
10 g / 2 tsp thyme
2 tbsp tomato concentrate

Clean the lobster heads with cold water. Mix the heads with the herbs and tomato on a baking sheet and bake for 30 minutes at 180°C (355°F) until golden. Pour it into a pot with the butter over medium-high heat until the butter starts boiling and turns brown. When the butter is about to burn, take it off the heat and strain it into another pot. Remove the foam with a large spoon so the only part left is the browned butter. Place in a container for future use.

ELDERFLOWER VINAIGRETTE

100 g / 3.5 oz elderflowers
600 g / 2½ cups vinegar
600 g / 1 lb 5 oz sugar
600 ml / 2½ cups water
18 g / 3.5 tsp Gellan
18 g / 3.5 tsp Citras
salt, to taste

Vacuum-pack the elderflowers and vinegar at least 2 months before the intended serving date. When ready, boil the vinegar with the sugar, water, Gellan, and Citras. Place in the refrigerator overnight until the mass is a large solid block of gel. Blend the block into a smooth gel and mix with an equal amount of the browned lobster butter. Add salt to taste.

PLATING
dried chamomile powder

Drain the pickled carrots, let them marinate in the elder-flower vinaigrette and dried cornflower petals. Arrange the "carrot spaghetti" into a shape of a ball to cover the grilled Norway lobster. Finally, dust with dried chamomile powder.

About the Dish

Here at Høst, we wanted to make a dish with grilled Norway lobster and have it taste of summer, so we used the preserved flowers from the previous summer. The idea originated from the colors yellow and orange.

Vækst – Copenhagen, Zealand, Denmark

Deep-fried chicken thighs and creamy pearl barley porridge with parsley and Vesterhav's cheese

Preparation

Serves 4

DEEP-FRIED CHICKEN THIGHS

800 g / 1 lb 12 oz good-quality chicken thighs
1 1/2 pt buttermilk
2 eggs
2 tbsp Dijon mustard
zest of 1 organic lemon
400 g / 14 oz wheat flour
400 g / 14 oz Maizena
5 g / 1 tsp fine salt
3 1/6 pt neutral oil, for deep frying
a pinch of vinegar powder, optional

Remove the bones and skin from the chicken thighs. Mix together the buttermilk, eggs, mustard, and lemon zest. Add the thighs and refrigerate for 1 hour. Meanwhile, mix together flour, Maizena, and salt in a bowl. Remove the chicken from the refrigerator and coat in the flour mixture. In a pot, heat the oil to 170°C (340°F). To ensure safe deep-frying, use a large pot (5–6 l / 10–12 pt).

Deep-fry the chicken thighs until golden and crispy. It takes about 4–5 minutes. Make sure that the chicken is cooked all the way through. When done, place the chicken on fat-absorbing paper, and lightly sprinkle with salt (and an especially light sprinkle of vinegar powder, if using).

CREAMY PEARL BARLEY PORRIDGE, PARSLEY, AND VESTERHAV'S CHEESE

500 g / 1 lb 12 oz organic pearl barley
500 g / 1 lb 1 oz mushrooms
300 g / 10.5 oz parsley, washed and cleaned
100 g / 3.5 oz baby spinach, washed and cleaned
100 g / 3.5 oz Vesterhav's cheese (or a hard Parmesan or manchego)
25 g / 5 tsp ramsons, finely chopped
25 g / 5 tsp enoki mushrooms
300 ml / 1⅓ cups cream, 38% fat
salt
lemon juice

Boil the barley in salted water until almost tender. Quickly douse with cold water. Set aside.

Rinse the mushrooms and place in a container or a casserole dish with 100 ml (½ cup) water. Cover to make an airtight seal. Bake in the oven for 1 hour at 160°C (320°F). Alternately, this can be done overnight at 80°C (175°F) to create a stronger, more flavorful stock. Finally, strain.

Boil the parsley in lightly salted water until tender. It takes about 3 minutes. Add the spinach at the end. Remove from boiling water and place in ice-cold water. Strain the water. Blend the spinach and parsley until smooth. Add salt to taste.

Mix the boiled barley, mushroom stock, and some of the cream in a pot. Bring to a boil. Add finely grated Vesterhav's cheese, salt, and lemon juice. Turn down the heat and let it simmer. Additional cream can be added.

The final consistency should resemble risotto. Mix the porridge with the parsley puree and finely chopped ramsons. Garnish with the raw enoki mushrooms.

PLATING
fresh juniper branches

Arrange the fried chicken on a nest of fresh juniper branches and serve the porridge in a deep plate on the side.

About the Dish

From pecking barley in the fields tended by humans to being served with barley and eaten by humans, this dish, served at Vækst, takes its inspiration from the life cycle of the chicken.

Jerusalem artichoke ice cream with caramelized apples, Jerusalem artichoke chips, and chocolate sauce with browned butter

Preparation

Serves 8

ICE CREAM

6 g / 1 tsp gelatin
350 g / 12 oz Jerusalem artichokes, peeled and cubed
50 g / ¼ cup butter
1 1/2 pt whole milk
200 g / 7 oz glucose
2 g / a pinch of salt

Soak the gelatin in cold water. Fry the Jerusalem artichokes in butter until golden and tender. Meanwhile, bring the milk, salt, and glucose to a boil. Add everything to a blender except for the gelatin. Blend until smooth. Strain and add the soaked gelatin. Place in the freezer.

CARAMELIZED APPLES

300 g / 10.5 oz sugar
50 g / ¼ cup butter
4 apples, peeled and cubed coarsely

Melt the sugar over low heat until golden. Then, add the butter, and when it has finished bubbling, add the apples. Now boil the apples in the caramel until tender. Cool a little and then blend.

JERUSALEM ARTICHOKE CHIPS

200 g / 7 oz Jerusalem artichokes, peeled and cleaned thoroughly
1 1/2 pt oil, for deep-frying

Use a mandolin to cut the Jerusalem artichoke into thin slices (chips).

Heat the oil to 150°C (300°F). Fry the chips until golden and crispy. Then, remove chips and place on fat-absorbing paper.

CHOCOLATE SAUCE WITH BROWNED BUTTER

200 ml / ¾ cup whole milk
100 g / 3.5 oz Jerusalem artichokes, peeled and cubed
100 g / 3.5 oz milk chocolate
100 g / 3.5 oz butter

Boil the milk and Jerusalem artichokes. Turn down the heat while maintaining a boil until the Jerusalem artichokes are tender. Strain the milk and discard the Jerusalem artichokes.

Brown the butter, whisking all the time, in a small pot over medium heat until golden.

Mix together the warm milk, milk chocolate, and browned butter. Stir until the chocolate has completely dissolved.

PLATING

Arrange the apple puree at the bottom of a flat plate and sprinkle with fried Jerusalem artichoke chips. Place a quenelle of ice cream in the chips and serve with the warm chocolate sauce at the table.

About the Dish

I have always loved to play with vegetables in desserts. So while this dish, served at Vækst, resembles a classic dessert with chocolate sauce, it breaks the traditional flavor pattern with Jerusalem artichoke.

BROR | Copenhagen, Zealand, Denmark

When René Redzepi tweeted, "just pure talent & huge balls" in a statement of encouragement for the former Noma sous chefs who had embarked on following their dreams and opened their own restaurant, he may not have envisaged such menu items as "Bull's balls with tartare sauce" or "Crispy dicks with ramson crème fraîche".

Victor Wågman
Samuel Nutter

– Head chefs & founders

While working side-by-side in the Noma kitchen we decided to open our own restaurant, and in 2013 we opened BROR, Danish for brother. We always knew we wanted to create an energetic and fun dining space that would be accessible to many, one that walked the fine line between comfort and culinary innovation.

We found an old restaurant space in central Copenhagen and, with help from our families, renovated everything from scratch. We could not afford expensive furniture or exclusive crockery back then; instead we found joy in choosing chairs and flatware from vintage stores. This mindset spread into all kinds of areas, especially in terms of developing the menu. It became a necessity to use all parts of our raw materials. What many might have regarded as trash, we turned into treasure: our dishes contain fish heads, cow uterus, even bull penis. It's a daily challenge to create something interesting from these products; at the same time, our everyday practices never turn into a routine when pushing the limits of what we can serve in our restaurant.

BROR – Copenhagen, Zealand, Denmark

Bull's balls with tartare sauce

About the Dish

Bull's balls was the original dish that led us to explore all the other less-known cuts and unused parts of animals. Given our very limited resources and our deviation from the products, such as oysters, lobster, and so on, that people commonly associate with a restaurant serving delicious food, we had to be extremely inventive in our approach. At the same time, we wanted to do something different in Copenhagen, and bull's testicles became the first step towards finding something that was unique to BROR.

Bull's balls are delicious in the way that their texture resembles sweetbread. We coat it with spiced breadcrumbs to add "warmth" and fry them so they are crispy on the outside, and nice and soft in the center. When you dip them in the mayonnaise-based tartare sauce, you are bound to get addicted. Fry them, try them—these balls are your guilty pleasure.

Preparation

Serves 6

BULL'S TESTICLE

1 bull's testicle
100 g / 3.5 oz flour
100 g / 3.5 oz egg yolk
100 g / 3.5 oz bread-crumbs

Blanch the bull's testicle in boiling water for 4 minutes and cool in ice water. Cut off the top and bottom of the testicles and run your finger between the flesh to loosen the membrane. Discard the membrane. Slice the flesh into 1 cm (0.4 in) slices. Set up 3 bowls: one for the flour, one for the egg, and one for the breadcrumbs. Dry the testicle slices and dust with the flour, dip them in the egg mixture, and then the breadcrumbs. Repeat the step with the eggs and breadcrumbs for a double layer.

MAYONNAISE

1 egg yolk
1 tsp mustard
300 ml / 1¼ cups grapeseed oil
salt
1 tsp white wine vinegar

Whisk together the egg yolk and mustard. Then slowly incorporate the oil, and season with salt and vinegar.

TARTARE SAUCE

20 g / 0.7 oz chopped shallots (pre-salted for 1 hour)
5 g / 1⅓ tbsp chopped parsley
50 g / 1.5 oz chopped cornichons
1 drop of lemon juice

Combine shallots, parsley, and cornichons with enough mayonnaise to bind it all together. Add a little lemon juice to round off the taste.

PLATING
500 ml / 2 cups frying oil

Fry the testicles until tender and golden brown on the outside. Make sure they stay juicy on the inside. Season with salt. Place a quenelle of tartare sauce on the plate together with the testicles.

Crispy dicks with ramson crème fraîche

About the Dish

If the penis of any animal had been served in a restaurant here 10 years ago, people probably would have reacted with great fear and disgust. However, since the public has been exposed to all sorts of unconventional foods during the last decade, such as heads, brains, livers, and sperm, we have come a long way in the acceptance of food. Getting bull penises delivered every day for 2 years, we worked on developing something delicious with them. We made stocks, soups, and salted purees before we realized we could serve them as "crispy dicks."

We figured we could change people's minds with this dish in particular: although disgusted at first, people are unexpectedly pleased after eating it. In that sense, the crispy dicks were our gateway to a new philosophy of using the less valued cuts to stimulate and change people's perception of what is considered delicious.

Preparation

Serves 6

DICK

1 dick
5% salt brine
1 1/2 pt water
500 g / 1 lb 1.5 oz
**   frying oil**
50 g / 1.7 oz salt

Put the dick into 5% salt brine overnight. On the following day, cook the dick in the simmering water until it is super tender (around 3 hours).

Take off the skin and membrane until all you have is the flesh. Roll up in cling wrap, cool, and then freeze. Remove from freezer, slice thinly, and dry overnight. Puff the slices in hot oil until the dick is crispy. Season with salt while warm.

DIP

20 g / 0.7 oz pickled
**   ramson capers**
200 g / 7 oz crème fraîche

For the dip, chop the ramson capers and stir with the crème fraîche.

PLATING

Place the dicks inside a bowl (or a crispy dicks package) and serve the crème fraîche in a separate small bowl so you can dip your dick.

CRISPY
DICKS

www.restaurantbror.dk

BR
OR

Glazed cow "vagina" smørrebrød

Preparation

Serves 6

UTERUS

1 cow uterus
2 tbsp grapeseed oil

Clean the uterus and vacuum-pack it with grapeseed oil. Cook for 24 hours at 80°C (175°F). Once cooked and tender, chill and slice.

MAYONNAISE

1 egg yolk
1 tsp mustard
300 ml / 1¼ cups grapeseed oil
salt
1 tsp white wine vinegar

Whisk together the egg yolk and mustard. Then slowly incorporate the oil, and season with salt and vinegar.

REMOULADE SAUCE

150 g / 5 oz cucumber
100 g / 3.5 oz green tomatoes
50 g / 1.5 oz yellow onions
50 g / 1.5 oz cauliflower
20 g / 1⅛ tbsp salt
50 ml / 1.5 oz water
90 g / 3 oz white wine vinegar
75 g / 2.5 oz sugar
10 g / 0.5 oz curry powder
15 g / 0.5 oz Colman's mustard powder
25 g / 1 oz wheat flour
10 g / 0.5 oz mustard seeds

Mince the cucumber, green tomatoes, onions, and cauliflower. Season well with salt and allow to drip overnight. On the following day, cook for 20 minutes in the water and 15 g (0.5 oz) of the white wine vinegar.

For the sauce, cook the remaining white wine vinegar with sugar, curry, mustard powder, and wheat flour for 10 minutes before straining. Then mix together the pickles and strained sauce and cook together for 10 minutes. Soak the mustard seeds in water and fold in at the end. Fold together equal quantities of remoulade base and mayonnaise for the finished remoulade sauce.

PLATING

1 tbsp reduced chicken stock (glaze)
3 tsp remoulade sauce
1 horseradish
1 red radish, sliced
1 small tray of cress
3 slices toasted rye bread

Crisp the uterus slice in a pan and brush with reduced chicken stock to glaze the meat. Spread the remoulade sauce on the toasted rye bread and place the meat on top. Grate the horseradish over the glazed meat, then place on top of the radish slices and finish with a sprinkling of cress.

About the Dish

Glazed beef *smørrebrød*—in Danish, literally "bread with butter"—has a long tradition here in Denmark. So this is a great example of adding something very unfamiliar to something very familiar. People can relate to it, yet they freak out at first when we tell them it is a "vagina." It is, however, their own repulsion transformed into satisfaction that ends up freaking them out the most when they realize how delicious this very powerful and dominant beef flavor truly is.

Nordic Food Lab
by Michael Bom Frøst & Roberto Flore

Nordic Food Lab was founded in 2008 with the mission to explore the culinary potential of the ingredients of the Nordic region and disseminate the results of this exploration to the world. The lab adopts and utilizes traditional and modern techniques from all over the world. The results of the lab's work are open-source and are continuously shared via a research blog on the website nordicfoodlab.org. Presently more than 150 posts are available. From November 2014, the lab has been located at the Department of Food, at University of Copenhagen. Prior to that, the lab's home was a houseboat situated in the harbour of Copenhagen, moored in front of Noma. Nordic Food Lab was founded by the gastronomic entrepreneur Claus Meyer and the head chef of Noma René Redzepi. They saw a need for the Nordic culinary world to have a lab that could experiment more and investigate a broader variety of techniques than a restaurant has the capacity to do. The investigations and experiments of the lab are fuelled by research, development, and dissemination grants from various government, non-profit sources as well as the commercial activities of the lab, such as consultancy and Anty Gin, the world's first gin flavoured with ants. Since January 2012, Michael Bom Frøst has been the director of the lab. Since June 2014, Roberto Flore has been working in the lab, first as head chef and from June 2016 with the title Head of Culinary Research and Development.

For much of history the yearly cycle of abundance and scarcity of food has been the fundamental pulse of life in the Nordic region. Over the centuries we have developed many methods and techniques to preserve food in times of plenty, to see us through the time of year when there is little food readily available. Fermentation is one of the key ingredients in these efforts to preserve food. Through this, chefs and later scientists and technologists have slowly built the capacity to evaluate what is optimal to do to preserve food and develop the flavours and textures that are the backbone of Nordic cuisine. The most fundamental rule of gastronomy is to make the best of what is available. There is a need to link gastronomy and science to develop a sound relationship with food and the edible world. A thorough understanding of the raw materials, from culinary, cultural and scientific perspectives increases the likelihood of success. Gastronomy is deeply rooted in both tradition and innovation. The culinary history is full of successful innovations that we now consider traditions. Access to new information is at the core of this. New connections, whether it was travellers or tradesmen, have given opportunities to explore novel raw materials and to learn novel techniques to preserve what is good to eat. Chefs' curious palates remain the main driver in their search for novel dishes, ingredients, and techniques.

At Nordic Food Lab we approach deliciousness with passion, precision, and the scientific method. The theoretical framework that we apply to get a comprehensive understanding of deliciousness is inspired by design theory. Our experience of a food occurs at three distinct levels: first, the basic, immediate sensory level is determined by how our senses are hardwired to transform the physical and chemical properties of food into a sensory experience. Second, food has the basic biological function of nourishing us; the nutrients we absorb from food fuel our bodies. Lastly, food has meaning and that is a large part of our appreciation of it. It may be that we like the methods by which the food is produced, or we admire a particular dish for its innovative content and its creative process. This reflective level is where the narratives work. Good narratives around the food we eat have the potential to change our food behaviors.

The idea of three distinct levels of interaction with food guides the creation of new foods and dishes at the lab. We have repeatedly found that when a food excels on all three levels, it is irresistible. A short description of how a food or

dish builds on tradition, or applies ancient techniques in novel ways, can provide a powerful weapon for those who seek to change the foodways of the world. In essence, good food is good for the senses, the body, and, not least, the mind. Deliciousness extends beyond the bodily pleasures a food provides.

Diversity is our starting point and the goal of our pursuits. For nature, diversity is not a luxury, it is a necessity. The selection of what to experiment with in our pursuit of deliciousness is rooted in the fact that it has to broaden the perspective of what we eat in the region. It has to expand the realm of what is considered edible, and to increase the diversity of what we eat. For our method of operation and experimentation, we rely on diversity in educational background and culture to ensure that we approach the development of new food in a multifaceted manner. We work in a similar manner to a design studio, relying on fast prototyping to move the development of ideas forward, and to develop many versions of the ideas. We constantly change perspective between a theoretical and a practical approach to food. We evaluate the outcome of experiments with our trained palates and systematic taste tests, and discuss ideas about how to elevate them to their highest potential.

MICHAEL BOM FRØST – *Copenhagen, Denmark*
Director, Associate Professor in Food Sensory Innovation

The Vision of the Forest
A dish by Roberto Flore

Using smells and aromas to introduce a new concept in a dish is something that has always fascinated me. Just imagine how many emotions and vivid memories a smell can generate.

Chemical compounds are part of the complex system of communication that plants, animals, and insects use. Most of the scents and flavors that are produced by living organisms are products of the interactions between these organisms within a given ecosystem. Chemical communication is a fascinating topic that requires intense study and knowhow and I have tried to explore this field from the point of view of a chef.

During the development of a new dish, we chefs combine taste, aroma, and textures in ways that give pleasure and create associations, but what happens if we try to unlock the complicated code of communication between living organisms?

The seeding idea for this dish came during fieldwork in Japan. We at the lab investigated the use of insects in local gastronomy, and as part of that we took part in a hunt for giant hornets, a type of hunting experience no less thrilling than that of hunting big game. I became intrigued by the concept of recreating the moment when we met the giant hornets during the hunt. It was a rainy day and fall was coloring the mountains with beautiful tones of red, orange, yellow, and green. Our friend Daisuke started digging the hornet nest from the ground. The hornets rushed out to meet the attacker, trying to bite, sting, and spray their venom. By emitting a strong smell into the air they released their message, communicating to the rest of the colony that their nest was under attack. The pungent venom of the giant hornets was, for me, one of the strongest memories of that day. By combining different scents on a plate would it be possible to tell a compelling story such as the one I had experienced in Japan?

Over the following days that idea just kept running through my mind, becoming an obsession. My goal was to design a dish that would tell the tale of an alphabet, secret to most humans, under the gastronomic spotlight.

The common wood ant, *Formica rufa*, sprays formic acid to defend its colony when it is under attack or has otherwise been disturbed. A strong perfume, reminiscent of citrus, can be detected in the air. Ants play a fundamental role in forest ecosystems; even though they appear insignificantly small, they are responsible for processes such as soil aeration and for destroying dangerous parasites, that can affect plants. How can recognizing that something is delicious change our perception of the natural world which surrounds us? Could such an approach create the basis for a more sustainable way of interacting with our environment?

I started to reflect on how it would be possible to describe this concept by using many elements from the forest but leaving the most important element invisible, the pure ant essence.

I use this dish to highlight the limitations that can stop us from deeply exploring the edible potential of our landscape and lead us as a result to undervalue some of the most remarkable wonders of the natural world. Attempts to change attitudes toward the increasingly insignificant value that our society places on biodiversity can start on a plate. Indeed, The Vision of the Forest provokes us to consider the relationships and interactions between different species and to try to place ourselves in an ecosystem in which we are not passive observers, but rather interpreters of the flavors and smells that we can experience while walking in a Nordic forest.

About the Dish

Immediately after returning from fieldwork in Japan, I spent a lot of time in the company of David Pedersen, a professional hunter and true nature enthusiast. We discussed the possibility of how hunting could be a practice through which to teach people how to approach meat consumption in a more integrated, responsible, and conscious way; perceiving ourselves as part of an ecosystem, rather than isolating ourselves from it. In other words, moving towards a more eco-centric notion of sustainable diets.

I was invited as a guest to a hunt in David's family's private forest. That day, I received three roe deer hearts as a gift from the hunting party—the perfect souvenir of this special occasion. I prepared two of them for the evening meal that night. As I was cooking, I remembered that I had brought a glass of grasshopper garum with me. I decided to serve the raw deer heart warmed up to body temperature and seasoned with some of the very first sprigs of ramson and a few drops of the garum. The third heart I brought back to the lab and started to compose this dish, The Vision of the Forest.

Endless choice is paralyzing. The limitations that geography and season place on us provide a creative straitjacket that gives traction to where to start and what to work with. Our mission is to increase diversity of foods in the Nordic larder. Our systematic method of working and evaluating ideas and results ensures that we continue to work to broaden the perspective of what good food is. The three-tiered theoretical framework for deliciousness tells us that in essence, good food needs to appeal not only to the senses and the body, but also to the mind of the eater. Deliciousness extends beyond the bodily pleasures a food provides, and into the narratives we construct about the foods that we desire.

ROBERTO FLORE – *Copenhagen, Denmark*
Head of Culinary Research and Development,
Nordic Food Lab, nordicfoodlab.org

The Vision of the Forest

Preparation

THE SUBSTRATE

- **40 g / 1.4 oz fermented mushroom paste**
- **4 g / 0.14 oz chanterelle powder**
- **15 g / 0.5 oz birch syrup**
- **3 g / 0.11 oz freeze-dried powder of beech leaves**
- **2 g / 0.07 oz green juniper berries**
- **1 g / 0.03 oz pine shoots**
- **8 g / ½ tbsp water**

Mix the ingredients and seal in a vacuum bag. Let sit overnight.

LIGHTLY CURED ROE DEER HEART

- **180 g / 6.4 oz roe deer heart**
- **20 g / 0.7 oz pine salt**
- **12 g / 0.4 oz birch syrup**
- **4 g / 0.14 oz green juniper berries**
- **5 g / 0.17 oz Anty Gin**
- **fresh herbs**
- **forest leaves**

Wash the heart in iced brine. Dry with a cloth and spray with some Anty Gin. Mix together salt, syrup, and juniper berries, and place mixture inside vacuum bag with the heart. Seal and leave in bag for 24 hours.

Remove the heart from the mix, clean, and smoke for 10 minutes with fresh herbs and leaves from the forest.

FERMENTED AND CRUNCHY ELDERBERRIES

- **2 g / 0.07 oz dried elderberries**

Prepare the wine with the elderberry flowers and then transform it into vinegar by adding the berries (see the recipe on our blog). Remove the berries from the liquid once it turns into vinegar. Place in the dehydrator at 65°C (150°F). Leave until dry.

BEAVER GLAND TINCTURE (CASTOREUM)

- **beaver castor sac**
- **70% tincture alcohol**
- **dried leaves**

Cover one beaver castor sac in 70% tincture alcohol. Leave for one month. (Castoreum is the secretion of the castor sacs of the Eurasian and North American beaver [*Castor fiber* and *Castor canadensis*, respectively]).

DRIED LEAVES

Freeze dry the leaves and cut in tiny pieces. Spray the leaves with castoreum 2 hours before serving.

ANT TINCTURE

- **10 formica rufa**
- **2 g / 0.07 oz pure ant distillate**

Infuse the ants with 40% ethanol in a rotovap. Freeze the rest of the ants and keep frozen until use.

PLATING

Brush the entire plate with the mushroom substrate. Cut the heart into small pieces. Place the rest of the ingredients on the plate, allowing three small bites of all the ingredients.

AOC

From both land and sea, chef Søren Selin focuses on the beauty of local raw materials. Located in the former cellar vaults of the seventeenth-century Moltke's Mansion, AOC is a sensory dining experience of refined, expertly crafted dishes paired with the wine selections of AOC founder, owner, and prized sommelier Christian Aarø.

Søren Selin

– Head chef & partner

I enrolled in culinary school at the impressionable age of 20. I made the decision so I could work with my hands and make some easy money, but it would unknowingly frame my future, as my fascination with the creative aspect of cooking grew. After graduating, I did what many young chefs did and moved to France to advance my culinary skills. But I truly began to be inspired, and to learn, upon returning to Denmark. During my time abroad, the culinary scene in Denmark had changed radically for the better. I worked for nine years at Alberto K, where I strived for a Michelin star—and voiced my vision—yet no cigar, so eventually I moved on. When I began working at the Michelin-starred AOC, I worked my utmost to defend it and challenged myself as a chef. Today I have two stars to defend at restaurant AOC. Accolades of great stature aside, my passion thrives on evolving as a chef in this world of endless culinary creativity.

My greatest source of inspiration is the produce itself. Sometimes, eager to showcase their skills, chefs stand in the way of the ingredient. For me, it is better to step back and serve dishes that allow the produce to take center stage. I have reached a point in my cooking where I no longer concern myself with what other chefs are doing. Sure, I am inspired by others, but there comes a time when a chef should just try things. That is the true moment of creation. Which, of course, remains a constant when working with the seasons. A new season brings new raw materials. It is gratifying to work with wild herbs, and biodynamic, wild, and organic produce. At the same time, it can be quite frustrating when your raw materials differ so much in shape and taste. You have to learn to work with what nature provides.

AOC – Copenhagen, Zealand, Denmark

Scallops with fermented asparagus and crown dill

Preparation

Serves 4

SCALLOPS AND FERMENTED ASPARAGUS

**4 live Norwegian scallops
fermented asparagus**

Open and clean the scallops in water. For curing the scallops, make a cure with salt and sugar by mixing two parts salt to one part sugar. Then, use 1.5% of the cure for the scallops (e. g. use 15 g cure per kilogram of scallops). Let the scallops cure for 3 hours. Blast freeze them individually.

Cut the scallops and fermented asparagus into very thin slices of equal length. Then assemble, one by one, a slice of scallop on top of a slice of fermented asparagus to resemble a rectangular-shaped terrine. Cut the edges off the "terrine" to make the sides perfectly even. Sprinkle with salt.

DILL OIL

**2 parts oil to 1 part
tarragon**

Blend together the oil and tarragon in a Thermomix until the mixture reaches 55°C degrees (130°F). Let rest with the pulp for 12 hours. Strain and hang in pastry bags to get rid of water.

STEAMED MUSSEL BUN

**5 g / 1 tsp dry yeast
340 ml / 1½ cups water
550 g / 2½ cups wheat flour
5 g / 1 tsp sugar
10 g / 2 tsp salt
5 g / 1 tsp apple vinegar
5 g / 1 tsp baking powder
50 g / 1.7 oz milk
25 g / 2 tbsp mussel
  powder**

Dissolve yeast in the water. Add the rest of the ingredients and spin for approximately 10 minutes at high speed. Spray the work surface with cooking spray (e. g. Babette). Weigh out 15 g (0.5 oz) dough per bun. Roll the buns, place in plastic mold, spray, and cover with cling wrap. Let rise for approximately 2 hours. Steam in the oven at 100°C (212°F) for 12 minutes.

MUSSEL CREAM, CROWN DILL SAUCE

Mix together cream and mussel juice, season with crown dill vinegar and salt.

PLATING

Place the "terrine" in the center of a deep bowl. Decorate with edible flowers (depending on the season) and pour the mussel cream, and crown dill sauce around the "terrine" of scallops and fermented asparagus.

About the Dish

I wanted to serve the beautiful, hand-dived Norwegian scallops raw. When you taste, touch, and feel a live scallop in the shell, there are some incredible textures. We then worked with asparagus from the sought-after farm of Søren Wiuff. He pickles them, and they are strong due to the fermentation process involving yeast, salt, and lemon juice. They pair well with schnapps, but I wanted to use them in a dish. In order not to overpower the taste of raw scallops, I sliced the fermented asparagus very thinly. It is kind of like a terrine, but there is no gelatin or anything binding it together. When the seasonal produce becomes available, this dish is often on the menu for a 2–3 week period.

Burned Jerusalem artichoke, hazelnut, and caramel

Preparation

JERUSALEM ARTICHOKE LEATHER

- 2.5 kg / 5 lb 8 oz Jerusalem artichokes
- 250 g / 9 oz of neutral oil
- 600 ml / 2½ cups white wine
- 400 ml / 1¾ cups water
- 5 g / 1 tsp salt
- 400 g / 1¾ cups sugar
- 18 g / 3½ tsps agar-agar

Wash the artichokes, and cut them in half. Boil until tender. Blend and cool down.

Add agar-agar to the cold artichoke puree while stirring. Bring to a boil for 1 minute. Cool down. Blend. Spread out and dry at room temperature.

HAZELNUT ICE CREAM

- 10 l / 10.5 qt cream, 9% fat
- 200 g / 7 oz glucose
- 2 kg / 4 lb 6 oz sugar
- 2.6 kg / 5 lb 12 oz roasted hazelnuts (180°C / 355°F for 20 minutes)
- 1 l / 4 cups pasteurized egg yolks
- 6 leaves gelatin

Mix together the cream, glucose, sugar, hazelnuts, and gelatin into a pot. Bring to a boil. Blend and strain. Emulsify with egg yolks until the mixture reaches 72°C (162°F). Strain and freeze.

CARAMEL

- 625 g / 1 lb 6 oz sugar
- 1.25 kg / 2 lb 12 oz milk
- 1.25 kg / 2 lb 12 oz cream
- 450 g / 16 oz egg yolk
- 325 g / 11.5 oz trimoline
- 10 sheets of gelatin
- 20 g / 5 tsp salt

Caramelize the sugar until dark golden brown. Bring the milk, cream, trimoline, gelatin, and salt to a boil. Pour over the caramel and dissolve completely. Cool down and emulsify with egg yolks until the mixture reaches 85°C (185°F). Strain.

PLATING (per plate)

- 1 tsp fresh Jerusalem artichoke, minced
- 2 tsp fresh hazelnuts, minced
- 3 tsp roasted hazelnuts, minced

Siphon a base of caramel onto the bottom of a wide-rimmed bowl. Place a scoop of hazelnut ice cream on top followed by the minced fresh Jerusalem artichoke, minced fresh hazelnuts and minced roasted hazelnuts. Then cover the bowl by fixing a piece of the round Jerusalem artichoke leather onto the rim. Finally, carefully burn a circle in the center with a torch until golden brown and crack a hole with a spoon to give a glimpse of what's hidden inside.

About the Dish

I am proud of this dish, which is the closest thing to what I would call a signature dish. Although it is not the most aesthetically pleasing, it is a representation of the way I want to prepare food these days. I cannot remember why, but the idea of working with artichoke leather got into my head. I struggled for a long time: rolling it up, spreading it out on a Silpat in a thinly layered sheet. It was too chewy and strange to bite. I then tried to burn it. Finally, I was happy to work with it: it became crispy and produced this wonderful aroma. To keep it crispy, I serve it cold. I now repeat this practice with a variety of root vegetables, depending on what is in season.

AMASS | Copenhagen, Zealand, Denmark

He's the chef and she's the host. Matt and Julie Orlando opened AMASS at Refshaleøen with a shared philosophy of holistic sustainability. The industrial feel of the harborside is embodied by the restaurant interior. The sounds of the Brooklyn underground bounce from the clad walls and polished concrete pillars as organic produce is picked from the restaurant gardens.

Matthew Orlando

– Head chef & co-founder

When I reflect on the mindset we had when we founded AMASS I can't help but feel a little guilty. In the beginning, we envisioned it as a restaurant that served guests. Of course, you are probably saying to yourself "yes, a restaurant is created to serve its guests," and you're right. Six months after we opened, I began to feel that something was missing, something that gave us a greater purpose. I realized that, if serving guests was the restaurant's only purpose, we were missing the bigger picture. I believe that a restaurant should be a platform for spreading a broader message.

We are now into our fourth year and I am proud to say that I feel we have found that purpose. We have set out on a journey that we hope will make an impact on both the restaurant industry and how people approach cooking every day.

I am happy to say that besides having reduced our carbon footprint drastically since the day we opened, we are doing something we truly believe in without losing sight of the bigger picture. Among other things, we examine all the by-products from our dishes and learn how to treat these items not as by-products, but as other products, as ingredients, rather than discarding them. We apply this process to everything: from preparing meals to running the restaurant on a daily basis. Hopefully, the generation after us can use the knowledge we leave behind to influence the generations to come.

AMASS – Copenhagen, Zealand, Denmark

Chewy carrots with almond "ricotta," tea leaves, and preserved elderflowers

Preparation

Serves 10

ALMOND "RICOTTA"

200 g / 7 oz almond pulp leftover from making almond milk
100 ml / ⅓ cup water
4 g / a pinch of salt
3 g / ½ tsp white wine vinegar
0.5 g / a pinch of xanthan gum

Place the almond pulp in a blender with the water, salt, white wine vinegar, xanthan gum. Blend on medium speed until all ingredients are emulsified together. Transfer to an airtight container and refrigerate for up to 3 days.

PRESERVED ELDERFLOWERS

1.1 l / 4½ cups water
500 g / 1 lb 1.6 oz sugar
300 g / 10.6 oz fresh elderflowers

In a saucepan, bring the water and sugar to a boil for 5 minutes. Cool in the refrigerator. Place the elderflowers and sugar water in a vacuum-sealed bag. Store at room temperature until bag starts to inflate slightly (approximately 4–5 days). Store in refrigerator for up to 1 year.

CARROTS

2 kg / 4 lb 6.5 oz large orange carrots
2 kg / 4 lb 6.5 oz large yellow carrots
2 kg / 4 lb 6.5 oz large purple carrots

Peel all the carrots and remove the stems. Cut 7 cm (2 ⅔ in) off the top of the thickest end of 5 carrots of each color. Using a mandolin, take the tops off carrots that are now left over and slice them into 1 mm (0.04 inch) pieces, keeping all individual colors separate. Reserve any scraps for juicing. Place all slices of carrots on perforated trays and steam at 100°C (212°F) for 6 minutes or until just tender. Remove the carrot slices from the trays and dry in a dehydrator for 1 hour at 61°C (141.8°F). Remove from the dehydrator and store each of the color groups in its own uncovered container at room temperature.

PICKLING LIQUIDS

75 g / 2.6 oz green tea leaves from last night's tea
75 g / 2.6 oz chamomile tea leaves from last night's tea
200 g / 7 oz 13% and 15% apple cider vinegar
1% salt brine

Juice all the remaining carrots separately. Place the different juices in separate pots and reduce by three-quarters. Remove from heat. Add 50 g (1.7 oz) moist green tea leaves to the reduced purple carrot juice, and add 20 g (0.7 oz) moist chamomile tea to the reduced yellow carrot juice. Let both steep for 4 minutes, then strain through a fine sieve separately into a blender. Blend on high until juice re-emulsifies with its solids. Cool in the refrigerator. Pour the orange carrot reduction into the blender and re-emulsify. Cool in the refrigerator. For the purple carrot reduction, add 13% apple cider vinegar to the reduction. Store in the refrigerator. For the yellow carrot reduction, add 13% apple cider vinegar to the reduction. Store in the refrigerator. For the orange carrot juice reduction, add 15% apple cider vinegar and 1% salt brine to the reduction. Store in the refrigerator.

CHEWY CARROTS

To rehydrate the carrots, place individually colored carrots in a container with a lid. Add just enough carrot pickling liquid to the corresponding dried carrots to coat. Imagine dressing a salad with vinaigrette. This should be done 1 hour prior to serving the dish.

PLATING

60 g / 2 oz toasted almond pieces
salt

Place a spoonful of the almond "ricotta" in the middle of a slightly concave plate. Cover it with the toasted almond pieces. Then, assemble a salad of intertwining carrot pieces over the "ricotta". Place small pieces of the preserved elderflowers on top of the carrots. Drizzle the excess orange carrot pickling liquid around the outside of the carrots. Finish by adding a few grains of salt on top of the carrots. Enjoy!

Hazelnut sorbet with coffee caramel, burned chocolate, and cep mushroom oil

Preparation

Serves 10

HAZELNUT SORBET

300 g / 10.6 oz hazelnut pulp (leftover from making hazelnut milk)
360 ml / 1⅝ cups water
54 g / 1.9 oz glucose
90 g / 3.2 oz trimoline
3 g / a pinch of salt

Spread a thin layer of hazelnut pulp onto a baking sheet. Bake in the oven at 160°C (320°F) until golden brown. Remove and let cool. In a medium saucepan, mix the water, glucose, and trimoline. Bring to a boil and keep boiling for 30 seconds. Remove and refrigerate. When hazelnut pulp and sorbet base have cooled, place them in a blender with the salt. Blend on high until smooth. Transfer the mixture to a Pacojet container and place in the freezer for at least 12 hours before spinning in the Pacojet machine.

COFFEE CARAMEL

500 g / 1 lb 1.6 oz leftover coffee
50 g / 1.7 oz trimoline
50 g / 1.7 oz glucose
100 g / 3.5 oz cream

Place the coffee, trimoline, glucose, and cream in a saucepan, and reduce total weight to 250 g (8.8 oz). Cool to room temperature and store. Any excess caramel can be stored in the refrigerator for up to 1 month.

BURNED CHOCOLATE

200 g / 7 oz 78% dark chocolate

Place the chocolate in a saucepan and cook until the temperature reaches 145°C (293°F). Pour over a flat tray and spread until 1 mm (0.04 in) thick. Place in the freezer overnight. The following day, break chocolate into pieces of approximately 9 cm (3½ in) diameter and put back into the freezer for at least 2 hours.

CEP MUSHROOM OIL

50 g / 1.7 oz dried cep mushrooms
200 g / 7 oz grapeseed oil

Place the mushrooms and grapeseed oil in a saucepan and bring to 80°C (176°F). Maintain that temperature for 1 hour. Remove from heat and let sit at room temperature overnight. The following day, strain the cep mushrooms and oil through a fine sieve. Place strained oil in a container and store in the refrigerator. Any excess oil can be stored for up to 1 month in the refrigerator (*Tip*: It is great for making your own mayonnaise.)

PLATING

Place the Pacojet container of hazelnut sorbet in the Pacojet machine and spin the desired amount. Place a scoop of hazelnut sorbet in the middle of the plate and drizzle it generously first with coffee caramel, then the mushroom oil. Place a large piece of the frozen burned chocolate over the top of the hazelnut sorbet and coffee caramel. Enjoy!

About the Dish

We have made a commitment to examining all by-products from our kitchen and to include at least one by-product in every dessert. We use two in this recipe: the leftover coffee from our pour-over coffee service as well as the hazelnut milk pulp.

It was 2 years of looking at a three-liter container of leftover coffee from service the night before that we finally figured out a way to process it back into the kitchen. Since then, coffee caramel has been a staple that keeps on reinventing itself.

The pulp left over from our nut milks still contains tremendous amounts of flavor. By roasting the pulp, the excess liquid from the milk process is removed and the flavor is concentrated. We add burned chocolate to cut through the otherwise rich, sweet dish with a touch of bitterness. The cep mushroom oil adds a savory note to balance out the dish. We hope this combination makes people think a little bit about what a dessert should be.

Pumpkin with black pumpkin skin and salted pumpkin guts

Preparation

Serves 10

BLACK PUMPKIN SKINS

**1 medium Prince Edward
  pumpkin (skins)
40 g / 1.4 oz honey
a pinch of salt**

Start saving pumpkin skins
6 weeks prior to preparing this
dish. Place 1 pumpkin's worth
of skins in a vacuum-sealed bag
and store in a dehydrator at
61°C (141.8°F) for 6 weeks. After
6 weeks, remove from bag. The
skins will be almost black and
extremely soft. Place three
quarters of the skins in a blender
and add just enough water
until it starts to spin. Add honey
and season with a little salt.
Refrigerate until ready to use.

BLACK PUMPKIN SKIN OIL
200 g / 7 oz grapeseed oil

Place the grapeseed oil and the
remaining black pumpkin skin
in a blender and pulse twice.
Transfer to an airtight container
and store at room temperature
for 24 hours. After 24 hours,
carefully spoon the oil off the
top. Try not to scoop up any
of the black pumpkin skin. Put
in refrigerator.

SOFT PUMPKIN

**1 medium Prince Edward
  pumpkin
black pumpkin skin oil**

Cut the skin away from the
pumpkin and reserve for making
black pumpkin skin for future
dishes. Halve the pumpkin and
scoop out the guts; reserve them
for making salted pumpkin guts.
Cut the pumpkin into 6 cm
(2⅓ in) wedges. Cut into
egg-shaped pieces with a sharp
paring knife. Place the pieces
into vacuum-sealed bags with
a spoon of black pumpkin skin
oil. Reserve the rest of the oil
for assembling the dish. Steam
at 100°C (212°F) for 30 minutes.
The goal is keep it from
becoming a pile of mush.
Basically, the pumpkin should
be slightly overcooked so it has
a custardy consistency but is
not too soft. When pumpkins
are finished cooking, transfer
the bags to an ice bath to cool
immediately. Remove from bath
and preserve pumpkins inside
the bags in the refrigerator.

SALTED PUMPKIN GUTS

**20 g / 0.7 oz dried red
  seaweed
2% salt brine**

When preparing pumpkins for
other dishes 5 days prior to
making this recipe, save all the
guts (i.e. seeds and connective
tissue) of the pumpkin that you
scoop out. Place the guts in a
blender and add just enough
water to make it spin. Remove
the mixture from the blender
and add 2% salt brine to the
guts and mix well. Place the
mixture in a vacuum-sealed bag
and store at room temperature
for 5 days. Note: It is okay if
the bag inflates a little. After
5 days, remove the guts from the
bag and place in a dehydrator
until they are fully dried
(approximately 12 hours). Blend
the dried pumpkin guts on
high with dried red seaweed
until everything becomes
a fine powder. Store at room
temperature. This spice mix
can be saved for up to 1 week
at room temperature.

PLATING

Heat a medium pot of water
and maintain the temperature
between 80°C and 90°C (176°F
and 194°F). Drop the desired
number of pumpkin pieces into
the water for 5 minutes. While
pumpkin pieces are heating,
place about 1 tablespoon of the
black pumpkin skin puree per
piece of pumpkin in a small
saucepan with a few drops of
water. Warm gently. Remove
the pumpkin pieces from the
bags and place on a holding
tray. Season with salt, then
generously cover with the
pumpkin guts powder. Place
each pumpkin piece in a bowl
and pour 1 tablespoon of
warm black pumpkin skin oil
around the pumpkin. Enjoy!

Frederikshøj | Aarhus, Jutland, Denmark

Set in the former staff lodge of the neighboring royal palace, Frederikshøj has an opulent dining room with floor-to-ceiling glass windows facing the dense treetops of Thor's Forest and the pristine bay of Aarhus. Chef Wassim Hallal's kitchen delivers elaborate, expertly manicured dishes with distinctive flavors at a consistently high standard.

Wassim Hallal

– Head chef & owner

Ever since I decided to become a chef, I had ambitions to be the best. Always setting high standards and goals for myself, I made a lot of sacrifices to achieve excellence, from being responsible only for myself during my early years at culinary school to here and now at Frederikshøj, where I am surrounded by a horde of talented chefs.

Nature and its rich diversity greatly inspire me and my creativity, as does my community of selected cooks committed to constant progress. As Voltaire once said: "Perfection is attained by slow degrees; it requires the hand of time."

We are always striving to be a bit better tomorrow, and this constant evolution makes it possible to deliver a memorable dining experience without any compromises on quality.

Potato "stones"

Preparation

Serves 10

MASHED POTATOES

- 300 g / 10.5 oz potatoes
- 15 ml / 1 egg yolk
- 20 ml / 4 tsp whole milk
- 5 ml / 1 tsp white wine vinegar
- 40 ml / 3 tbsp olive oil
- 5 g / 1 tsp salt
- 50 g / 1.75 oz smoked salmon

Boil the potatoes until tender and let them steam off. Mash the potatoes in a Varimixer and add the other ingredients. Chop the salmon into fine pieces. Finally blend in the salmon pieces, shape into stones and place in the freezer.

POTATO SOUP

- 100 g / 3.5 oz potatoes
- 50 g / 1.75 oz onions
- butter
- 100 ml / ⅓ cup milk
- 100 ml / ⅓ cup cream
- 50 ml / ¼ cup water
- 1.4 g / a pinch of salt
- 3.5 g / 0.1 oz agar
- 0.5 g / a drop of black dye
- 4 g / 1 tsp white dye

Sauté the onions and potatoes in a little butter until golden. Add the milk and cream, and boil the potatoes until tender. Mix the soup with the water and salt. Bring to a boil with the agar, white food dye and half of the black dye. Marble the mass with the second half of the black dye, then dip the potatoes in.

PLATING

Arrange the finished "stones" on real stones to trick your guests.

About the Dish

I love to imitate: to create something that looks like something it is not. I had been working on the "stones" for several years before they succeeded. And, of course, they are made from something that is wonderfully and traditionally Danish: potatoes as the main base and smoked salmon to add flavor.

"Cherries"

Preparation

CHERRY GEL

**100 ml / ⅓ cup
cherry juice
1.2 g / a pinch of agar**

Bring the cherry juice to a boil
with the agar. Let cool and blend.

CHERRY MOUSSE

**10 g / 2 tsp cherry gel
5 g / 1 tsp whipped cream**

Stir the gel and cream together.

CHERRY SORBET

**100 ml / ⅓ cup cherry
juice
30 g / 2 tbsp sugar**

Bring the juice and sugar to
a boil. Let cool, then process
in an ice cream machine.

ALMOND MACARON

**22.5 g / 0.8 oz marzipan
20 g / 4 tsp sugar
8 g / ½ tbsp egg whites**

Whip the ingredients together.
Shape into macarons, and bake
in a preheated oven at 160°C
(320°F) for 12 minutes. Crush
when the macaron is cold.

CARAMEL "BEADS"

**500 g / 1 lb 1.5 oz sugar
5 g / 1 tsp glucose
red food dye**

Boil the sugar and glucose at
120°C (250°F). Set aside
a small portion for the stems.
Dye the mass until cherry red.
Then form the caramel "beads"
with an appropriate sugar
pump. Shape "stalks" from
the reserved caramel.

PLATING

Gently inject the sorbet
into one "cherry." Fill the
second "cherry" with
the gel, mousse and
macaron layer by layer.
Neatly place the two
"cherries" on a plate and
attach the "cherry stalks."

About the Dish

I love to play with caramel and
the season was ideal for cherries.
So it was natural for me to create
edible "cherries" made of sugar
and fill them with actual cherries
with different textures.

Gastromé | Aarhus, Jutland, Denmark

Half throttle, full throttle or signature? Gastromé serves up its cuisine as a 5-, 10- or 13-course set menu. Within arm's reach is Gastromé's primary source of inspiration, whether it be the neighboring forests or a relative's wild watercress garden. The result: creative, complex cooking with uncompromised delivery.

Søren Jakobsen & William Jørgensen

– Founders, restaurant manager & head chef

Making good food that makes people happy is what keeps us going! Our journey has been shaped by working inside and outside of Denmark for the past 20 years, working in new places, making them successful, and continuing to put energy and passion into those places. It's the people who have had the biggest impact on shaping our journey.

The local gastronomic stage has welcomed us and elevated our growth and expansion, providing us with many opportunities to develop our culinary expression, and this has really shaped our direction and pro-gression. One of the highlights, of course, was receiving our first Michelin star in February 2015. The most rewarding accolade, however, is when our guests acknowledge our staff for the great job we're doing. We are always trying to develop both our staff and ourselves. We believe that every little detail matters when cooking; you have to pay attention to all the steps in the process. When you achieve a flawless result, it is almost a magical feeling. On such nights you can notice a special buzz taking over the kitchen and we cannot compare that feeling to anything else!

Gastromé – Aarhus, Jutland, Denmark

Halibut confit with Jerusalem artichokes and wild watercress

Preparation

Serves 2

HALIBUT CONFIT

**350 g / 12.5 oz halibut
fillet
200 ml / ¾ cup oil
salt, to taste**

Add a thin layer of salt to the
fillet and put the halibut in the
refrigerator for 2–3 hours. Put
the oil and the fish in a vacuum
bag and vacuum on low using
the vacuum sealer. Set the
sous-vide to 46°C (115°F) and
cook the fish sous-vide for
15–20 minutes, depending on
thickness. Remove the halibut
from the heat and refrigerate
overnight. The next day, remove
the halibut from the bag and
dry off the excess oil. Cut the
halibut into thick slices.

LEMON CONFIT

**3 lemons
100 g / 3.5 oz sugar
½ Bora Bora vanilla pod**

Peel the zest off the lemons
without the white part. Remove
and discard the white pith. Cut
out all the fillets, reserving the
juice. Blanch the lemon zest
7 times in boiling water, using
fresh water each time. Cook
down the zests, fillets, and
lemon juice with sugar and
vanilla. When heavily reduced,
put the lemon confit into a
blender and blend until smooth.
Add a little salt and sugar if
needed—the taste should be
quite acidic and fresh.

JERUSALEM ARTICHOKE
CRUDITÉ

**4 big Jerusalem
artichokes
½ tsp baking powder**

Peel the Jerusalem artichokes
and cut them into very thin
slices. Put the slices in iced water
with baking powder and dry
quickly before plating.

JERUSALEM ARTICHOKE
PUREE

**200 g / 7 oz Jerusalem
artichoke
200 ml / 1 cup whole milk
salt, to taste**

Peel the Jerusalem artichoke
and cook until tender in the
milk. Strain the artichokes
and blend in the blender until
smooth. Add salt to taste and
a little extra of the cooked milk
if needed.

KOHLRABI
1 kohlrabi

Peel the kohlrabi and cut into
long thin strips with a Japanese
mandolin. The strips need to
be 2 × 12 cm (0.75 × 4.75 in).

WATERCRESS SAUCE

**2 bunches wild
watercress
1 garlic clove
2 avocados
1 1/2 pt vegetable stock
100 g / 3.5 oz chopped leek
salt and pepper, to taste**

Put the wild watercress in
a blender. Then add the garlic,
leek, and avocados, and blend
with the vegetable stock until
smooth and dark green. Add salt
and pepper to taste and strain
the sauce through a chinois.

WATERCRESS OIL

**100 ml / ⅓ cup
rapeseed oil
200 g / 7 oz wild
watercress**

Blend the oil and watercress in
a Thermomix on high speed at
60°C (140°F) for 10 minutes.
Strain through a fine chinois.

BUTTERMILK SAUCE

**200 ml / ¾ cup
buttermilk
1½ lemons
100 ml / ½ cup
heavy cream
salt and pepper, to taste**

Mix together the buttermilk and
lemon juice, and add salt and
pepper to taste. Whisk the cream
to a smooth and fluffy texture
and mix in with the buttermilk
to a creamy consistency.

PLATING

Dress the course with fresh
wild watercress.

French quail with chanterelle, yellow beets, and reindeer moss

Preparation

Serves 2

QUAIL CRÉPINE WITH MORELS

- **150 g / 5.5 oz chicken breast**
- **salt**
- **2 eggs**
- **200 ml / ¾ cup heavy cream**
- **100 g / 3.5 oz chopped morels**
- **2 quails**
- **100 g / 3.5 oz fat netting**

Slice the chicken breasts into small cubes and put them in a food processor with salt, and mince until smooth. Gradually add the eggs. Slowly add the heavy cream and blend until smooth. Then, add the chopped morels and fold it together with a spatula. Debone the quail breast and thigh—more precisely, debone the quail thigh at the upper part and release the lower part so you end up with a "drumstick" without bones. Put the caul fat on a cutting board and place thigh on it. Spread the chicken mixture on the thigh and place the quail breast on top. Wrap the caul fat tight around it. Roll the crépine tight in cling wrap so it looks like an ice cream cone. Leave the meat to firm up in the refrigerator for a couple of hours and then poach them for 14 minutes in water.

FRIED CHANTERELLES

- **150 g / 5.5 oz chanterelles**
- **1 finely chopped shallot**
- **butter, for frying**
- **salt, to taste**

Fry the chanterelles in a hot pan. Add the shallot and finish with butter and salt.

CHANTERELLE PUREE

- **1 chopped shallot**
- **100 g / 3.5 oz chanterelles**
- **1 sprig of thyme**
- **salt, to taste**
- **200 ml / ¾ cup heavy cream**
- **1 tbsp butter**

Fry the shallots and chanterelles in a pan with the thyme. Add the butter and sauté until the butter starts to brown. Add the cream and reduce by half. Blend everything and add salt. Strain through a fine mesh sieve.

MUSHROOM SOIL

- **200 g / 7 oz button mushrooms**
- **70 g / 2.5 oz malt flour**
- **100 g / 3.5 oz wheat flour**
- **200 g / 7 oz almond flour**
- **25 g / 5 tsp sugar**
- **2 tbsp dark beer**
- **salt**

Blend the button mushrooms with malt and wheat flour. Add the paste to a tray and bake until crispy at 180°C (355°F). Let cool. Then blend the crispy paste, add almond flour, sugar, beer, and salt, and dry in the oven at 100°C (210°F) for 30−45 minutes.

PICKLED AND GLAZED YELLOW BEETS

- **250 g / 8.75 oz yellow beets**
- **100 g / 3.5 oz sugar**
- **100 ml / ⅓ cup apple cider vinegar**
- **100 ml / ⅓ cup water**
- **1 tbsp black peppercorns**
- **3 tbsp honey**
- **6 tbsp butter**
- **1 tbsp water**
- **salt**

Bake the yellow beets for an hour at 160°C (320°F) and peel them. Bring the water, sugar, and vinegar to a boil and add the beets and peppercorns. Leave the beets to pickle for a couple of days. Bring the honey, butter, and water to a boil and emulsify with a blender. Cut the beets into cubes and glaze them in the syrup.

CONFIT POTATOES

- **2 big baking potatoes**
- **200 ml / ¾ cup duck fat**
- **salt, to taste**

Peel the potatoes and cut them into 2 cm (0.8 in) slices in length, then cut them into drop shapes. Lightly salt the potatoes and leave them to rest in a bit of water for 20 minutes. Remove the potatoes from the water and add them to the hot duck fat; let them confit in the oven at 160°C (320°F) for about 10−15 minutes, depending on the type of the potatoes.

FRIED REINDEER MOSS

- **160 g / 5.5 oz reindeer moss**
- **oil**
- **salt, to taste**

Clean the reindeer moss with tweezers and wash it in cold water. Put the moss to dry on a towel. Heat up the oil to 160°C (320°F) and fry the reindeer moss for a few seconds in the oil. Salt to taste.

SALMIS SAUCE

- **500 ml / 1 pt homemade veal jus/chicken stock**
- **500 ml / 1 pt apple juice**
- **500 ml / 1 pt white wine**
- **6 ripe tomatoes**
- **4 Danish Belle de Boskoop apples**
- **2 sprigs thyme**
- **100 g / 3.5 oz cold butter**
- **salt and pepper**

Bring the stock, apple juice, and white wine to a boil in a casserole dish. Cut the tomatoes and apples into small pieces and add them to the sauce with the thyme. Cook the sauce until it has reduced by half. Pour the sauce through a strainer and reduce it again to 300 ml (1¼ cup). Add salt and pepper, and emulsify with the cold butter before serving.

PLATING

Dress the course with fried reindeer moss and red oxalis.

Alchemist | Copenhagen, Zealand, Denmark

Molecular gastronomy meets a SOHO nightclub in an eerie museum—the fantasy of Rasmus Munk. Draw back the curtains of restaurant Alchemist to find provocative, transcendent, theatrical dining. Expect the unexpected, yet rely on an uncompromising commitment to taste, quality, and consistency served by Rasmus himself in an intimate, 15-seat culinary paradise.

Rasmus Munk

– Head chef & founder

Fine dining was definitely not a part of my upbringing in the small city of Randers in Jutland. At my house, béarnaise sauce was made from Knorr powder and dinner most nights consisted of frozen pizza. Honestly, I was more likely to spend my days fixing people's cars than their meals. After finishing school, I followed a friend of mine toward a culinary education simply because I had nothing else to do. My friend soon dropped out but I was absolutely hooked. The school opened my eyes to a whole new world of techniques, tastes, and the basic principles of cooking. I remember the first time I was asked to do a simple vinaigrette for a green salad; I thought the teacher was joking when he told me to put olive oil on the iceberg salad. I was fortunate enough to encounter some brilliant chefs, both at school and later on. They taught me about taste and the powers of the meal, opened my eyes to different food cultures, and pushed me just enough to keep me motivated and continue learning.

Challenges have always driven me forward. During school I participated in several competitions and I absolutely loved it! Since I opened Alchemist, the ultimate challenge for me has been to keep on pushing the limits of the meal. There is no fun in doing what everybody else does. Therefore, I find a lot of my inspiration outside the kitchen in social and political issues that move me. For me the ultimate dining experience is not only delicious, it is also thought-provoking, sends a message, and might even make a small change in the guest's life.

Lamb brain

About the Dish

When killing an animal, the least you can do is respect it enough to use it all, nose to tail. With this dish, I would like to challenge people's perception of what you can and cannot eat. Despite being abundant in nutrition and high in fat (it is comparable to foie gras), brain is seldom seen on the menu nowadays. Alchemist was actually the first Danish restaurant to be approved to serve lamb brain. I would like to bring back the use of guts in restaurants and home cooking. They are delicious, often cheaper than the first cuts, and abundant in taste and nutrition.

When I first started working with lamb brain, I was very surprised to find how rich it was in nutrients and fat. That inspired me to create a mousse similar to the well-known foie gras mousse. However, I still wanted to remind the guest about the origin of the dish and therefore plated it inside a lamb's skull. Each skull is extensively cleaned before it is used for serving. The mealworms add an additional layer of surprise and provide a much-needed crunchiness to an otherwise smooth, creamy dish.

Preparation

Serves 4

LAMB BRAIN MOUSSE

500 g / 1 lb 1.5 oz lamb brain (or foie gras)
200 g / 7 oz foie gras
fine salt and ground pepper, to taste
50 ml / ¼ cup soya

Poach the lamb brain in lightly salted water for 2 minutes and mash through a sieve until a homogeneous puree is achieved.

If you are using foie gras instead, take it out of the refrigerator and leave it at room temperature for about 4 hours before mashing. Taste and adjust with soya, salt, and pepper.

MEALWORMS

100 g / 3.5 oz mealworms
10 g / 2 tsp curry powder
fine salt, to taste

Toast the mealworms in a pan until golden and crunchy. Toast the curry powder in a dry pan. Season the mealworms with curry powder and salt to taste.

LEMON THYME AND LEMON ANTS

1 bundle fresh lemon thyme
10 g / 2 tsp fresh lemon juice
ants (or 1 finger lime)
100 ml / ⅓ cup nitrogen

Set aside lemon thyme leaves for decoration later. Freeze the ants in liquid nitrogen, after which they are ready to be served. If you are using finger limes, cut and squeeze out the little lime pearls. Note: If you don't have liquid nitrogen, freeze the ants for an hour in the freezer beforehand.

"BRAIN SHELL"

200 g / 7 oz vinegar powder
410 g / 14.5 oz lactose
110 g / 4 oz powdered milk
30 g / 1 oz egg white powder
60 g / 2 oz freeze-dried garlic powder
5 g / 1 tsp fine salt
25 g / 5 tsp onion powder
275 ml / 1¼ cups water

Stir all the ingredients together until a homogenous mass is achieved, then spread it on a silicone mat. Dry the mass in the oven at 60°C (140°F) for 24 hours. The "brain shells" are then cut out with a cutter in a suitable shape.

PLATING

Arrange the lamb brain mousse on 4 plates and decorate with lemon thyme leaves, lemon ants, and mealworms. Finally, place a "brain shell" on top of the crème. Serve with bread.

To serve the lamb brain like Alchemist, plate the ingredients inside the skull of the lamb, which has been cleaned for 3 months, and let the mealworms "crawl" out.

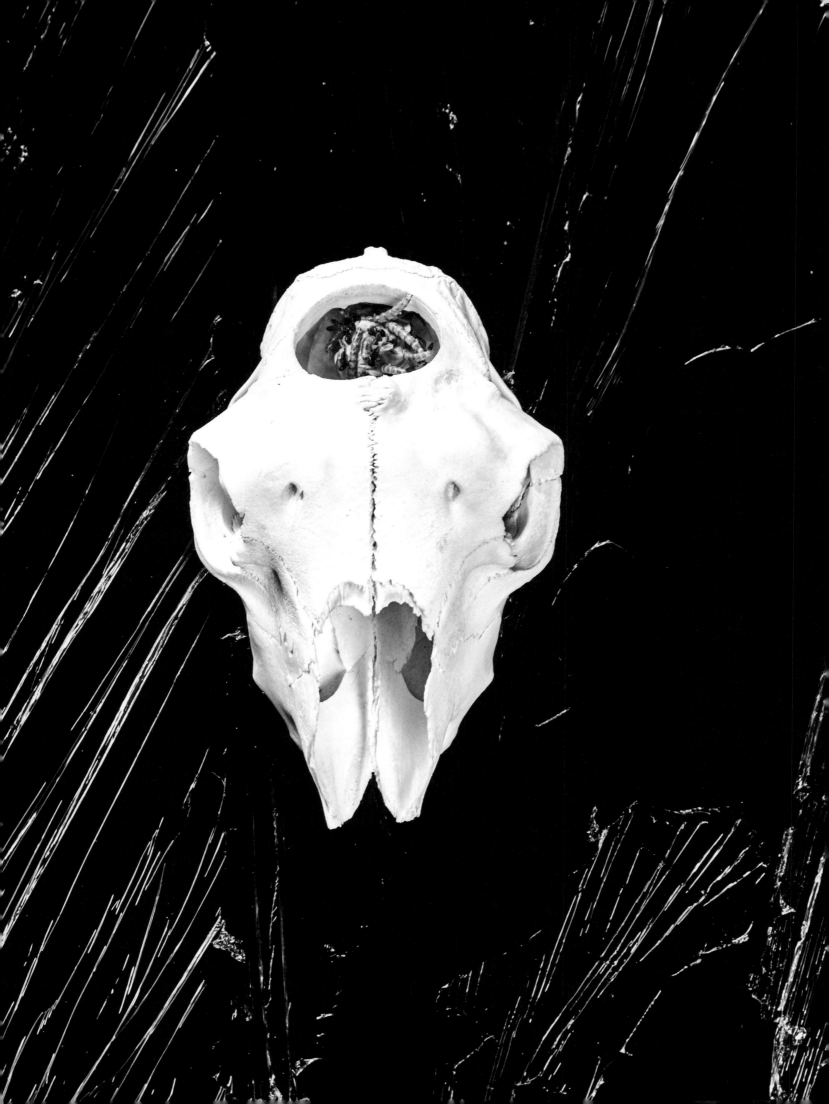

Lamb heart tartare

About the Dish

My inspiration for this dish does not come from the culinary world, but instead from a grim number: in 2016, 29 people in Denmark died while waiting for an organ. Those without an organ donor inspired me to develop this dish, which is served with a donor card. Whether one wishes to donate an organ or not is a personal affair, but it should be an active opt-in or opt-out. This dish encourages our guests to take a side.

Humor is often the best way to approach issues that can be hard to speak about, so we serve the sauce in a blood transfusion bag coiled on a transfusion rack. It always brings a smile to our guests' faces.

Since the dish was to focus on organ donation, we knew we would be working with blood and internal organs. But I had actually not worked much with blood before. In the old days, blood was used for several dishes, but unfortunately one does not very often encounter blood in cooking anymore. I spent a while researching the different ways blood can be used and I became fascinated by how coagulated blood can be used as a thickener. It became the basis for the dish.

Preparation

Serves 4

TARTARE

- **400 g / 14 oz lamb heart (or ox top round)**
- **60 g / 2 oz tomato puree**
- **90 g / 3 oz mayonnaise**
- **24 g / 1½ tbsp Dijon mustard**
- **45 g / 3 tbsp minced capers**
- **45 g / 3 tbsp minced cornichons**
- **6 g / 1 tsp salt**
- **20 ml / 1⅓ tbsp cognac**

Hollow out the lamb heart while preserving the "shell". Refrigerate the "shell" immediately. Remove excess fat and sinews from the meat, then cut it into small cubes (5 × 5 cm / 2 × 2 in). Mix in all the other ingredients, except for the cognac, until a homogeneous mass has been formed. Then add the cognac little by little and turn the meat in the sauce.

BLOOD SAUCE

- **500 g / 1 pt cherry juice**
- **1 l / 2 pt chicken stock**
- **150 g / 5 oz lamb blood**
- **salt and pepper, to taste**

Reduce the cherry juice to about half the total volume over low heat. Then, add it to the chicken stock and reduce again to half its volume. Add the blood while stirring (still on low heat). Cool the sauce to approximately 16°C (60°F).

PLATING

The tartare is served in the shell of the heart on crushed ice. As an alternative, you can arrange the tartare on a plate. Gently pour the blood sauce on the heart when serving at the table.

No.2 | Copenhagen, Zealand, Denmark

Founded by Christian Aarø and Søren Selin, No.2 embodies a simplified approach to their acclaimed restaurant AOC. Situated on the canal of Christianshavn and overlooking the polished granite cladding of the Black Diamond mirroring the sea, No.2 offers high-quality, seasonal delicacies under the direction of chef Nikolaj Køster.

Nikolaj Køster

– Head chef

No.2 opened its doors in June 2014. The restaurant's aim is to reflect the Nordic Kitchen, and at the same time be a pendant to AOC.

    With a background in banking, I first attended culinary school at the age of 24. I longed for something more creative and cooking had always fascinated me. After finishing my apprenticeship, being part of achieving a Michelin star at AOC, and working at other restaurants like Umami, Kokkeriet, and Pluto, I returned to my roots when Christian Aarø, owner of AOC, opened the little sister restaurant, No.2.

    At No.2, we get a lot of our inspiration from the small producers we work with. It is usually with them that we can find more unique products;

they give us special insights into where the products come from and how they come to be. It can be anything from the meat we use to the herbs that transform the dishes we make into something special. It is a good way to find inspiration for the dishes and something that defines us as a restaurant.

    For me, it is important that our guests can tell there is a firm idea behind the dish and that it clearly reflects our Nordic environment. There doesn't, however, need to be a recognition of value in each dish. I just think it is important that you can surprise guests by creating something unexpected.

No.2 – Copenhagen, Zealand, Denmark

Aged beef tartare with ramson

Preparation

Serves 4

RAMSON OIL

500 g / 1 pt plant oil
250 g / 9 oz ramsons

Blend at 70°C (160°F) for about 5 minutes. Let cool, then strain.

RAMSON EMULSION

120 g / 4 oz egg whites
8 g / 0.3 oz salt
30 g / 1 oz apple cider vinegar
270 g/ 1 cup ramson oil

Blend all ingredients together.

ONION ASH
10 large yellow onions

Arrange the onions. Cut into shells on a baking sheet, and roast in the oven at 180°C (355°F). Remove from oven when completely black and let cool. Blend to a fine powder. The above is to be made in advance and used in the recipe below.

TARTARE

280 g / 10 oz hand-cut tartare (beef inner thigh)
salt

Remove tendons and membranes from meat. Cut the meat into small cubes and marinate in the ramson oil and salt.

BURNED ONION COMPOTE

4 spring onions
plant oil
salt
4 g / a pinch of onion ash

Cut the spring onions into rough slices and wash them thoroughly. Coat in plant oil and burn with a gas torch until they gain some color. Add ramson oil, salt and onion ash to taste.

RAMSON CAPERS

10 g / 0.5 oz ramson capers
salt

They have a short season and there is a high demand for them, so get a lot if you have the opportunity.

Prepare the capers. Place them in salt for two days and store in a pickle marinade.

PLATING

40 g / 1.5 oz ramson emulsion
100 g / 3.5 oz burned onion compote
10 g / 0.5 oz chopped shallots
20 springs European sea rocket
4 g / a pinch of onion ash

Position five small caps of ramson emulsion on the plate. There should be 1 cm (0.04 in) between each cap. Then, arrange the burned onion compote on top of the emulsion with the finely chopped shallots. Marinate the meat with the ramson oil and season with salt. It should be arranged so that the meat finely covers the other elements on the plate. Decorate with ramson capers and sea rocket on top of the meat. Lastly, sprinkle a little onion ash over the dish and it will be ready to serve.

About the Dish

I wanted to create a tartare where you got the feeling of really eating something raw! The meat is from a small organic farm in Varde Ådal in Jutland. After the slaughter, the meat is matured for four weeks to enhance the flavor and texture. We have chosen to cut the meat to emphasize the idea of it being raw. Even though it is a stirred tartare, it has a menacing look because the meat is fashioned to cover most of the dish. The main idea is to bring Nordic nature into the dish. Because of this, we have incorporated a variety of onions and herbs; in particular, ramson and European sea rocket add unique Nordic flavors.

Plum dessert

Preparation

Serves 4

FERMENTED PLUM FOR SORBET

625 g / 1 lb 6 oz pitted plums
207.5 g / 7 oz sugar

Mix together and vacuum-pack at 90%. Let sit at room temperature for 2 days or until the fermentation is complete. Put it into the oven at 80°C (175°F) with steam in order to prevent the bag from breaking.

SORBET BRINE

612.5 g / 2½ cups water
25 g / 0.8 oz glucose
140 g / 5 oz dextrose
462.5 g / 1 lb sugar
7.5 g / 0.25 oz melatin

Boil the water and glucose in a pot. Mix together all the dry ingredients in a bowl and add to the water while stirring. It is important to let it boil, then let it cool. It will set like a jello.

FERMENTED PLUM SORBET

500 g / 1 lb 2 oz sorbet brine
425 g / 15 oz fermented plums
82.5 g / ⅓ cup water

Blend together and sculpt on a Pacojet tube.

MALT CRUMBLE

250 g / 9 oz sugar
250 g / 9 oz butter
150 g / 5.5 oz malt flour
250 g / 9 oz flour

Stir everything together in a food mixer. Bake the crumble for 30 minutes at 140°C (285°F). Bake for an additional 30 minutes at 120°C (245°F). Let cool.

PLUM SLICES
1 ripe plum

Cut the plum into crescent moon shapes and use for decoration.

WHITE CHOCOLATE CREAM

400 g / 1¾ cup milk
150 g / 5.5 oz cream
100 g / 3.5 oz white chocolate
90 g / 3 oz sugar
90 g / 3 oz egg yolks
50 g / 1.75 oz corn flour
100 g / ⅓ cup milk
50 g / 1.75 oz cold butter

Warm the milk, cream, white chocolate, and sugar in a saucepan. Whisk together the egg yolks, corn flour, and milk in a large saucepan. Pour the warm milk mixture over the egg yolk mixture. Place the mixture back on the stove until it has thickened. Whisk in the cold butter.

PLUM PUREE

Deseed the plums. Warm them up and blend until you have a smooth puree.

PLATING

Place a small spoonful of plum puree next to an equal-sized spoonful of white chocolate cream. The sorbet is arranged as a quenelle to the side of the two other elements. The sorbet is then slightly flattened with the underside of a spoon. Plum slices are placed nicely to the side of the sorbet and on top of the puree and chocolate cream. Finally, sprinkle the malt crumble over the dish.

About the Dish

I believe we have some of the most amazing plums here in Denmark. Unfortunately, the plum season is very short, so it is very important to have prepared a good dish when the plums are ripe. We have experimented a lot with fermentation, which has resulted in many new and unique flavors of food that we already know. We found it interesting to use this flavor in a sorbet along with the malt and fresh plums.

Toe to Toe with the Ant Man
by Thomas Laursen

How were you first introduced to a life of foraging? At the impressionable age of five, I collected oysters and mussels in Normandy, France. This would guide my search for wild foods for years to come—hunting for delicious food was just an amazing thing for me. From then I went on, mainly on my own, to discover nature, acquiring the skills necessary for a learned forager.

How do you know what all these plants are? It took 25 years to acquire the knowledge I have today. I worked constantly within the intricate puzzle of foraging, and used various tools and references, such as books, people, studies, academia, new knowledge, international publications, and chemists. Foraging is no new concept; it has been done for ages. These, however, are new times, and knowledge is passed on at an increasingly rapid rate. I read, listen, look, taste, check, double-check. There is no university or book that can do it all—it is a puzzle.

Your business model of supplying restaurants with wild foods—how did that begin? I had been cooking with wild food for quite some time. I started out doing a very small-scale supply to some local restaurants. When Noma opened it doors and broadened the subject of food diversity, the interest in wild food grew stronger and stronger. Somewhere along the way I offered wild black trumpet mushrooms to Noma, got in contact with them and educated them about this unique type of ant, the orange carpenter ant. I used my homemade apparatus to suck the ants from the tree and ship them live to Noma, where they incorporated them into a dish and served them semi-chilled. It was then I became known as the Ant Man! Overnight, I started my business Wildfooding, building it up bit by bit, helping, inspiring, and supplying Denmark's best restaurants.

Were there predecessors in the industry who inspired you before you started? Without Roland Rittman there would be no Wildfooding, maybe even no Nordic kitchen at the level we are at today. I owe him a great deal. I also looked to England: I am inspired by my friends Miles Irving and John Wright. Today I have friends and foragers working with wild food all over the world and sharing the knowledge on the endless search for *Vild Mad*.

What are the primary functions of your wild foods business, how does it work, and what do you do? I do many different things today. I am so fortunate that I can run my business while doing a variety of activities. I forage and supply, I write books, I do talks and give guided forage walks, even some on TV. I am involved in various projects to further share the knowledge of wild food through numerous festivals, products, and more.

Do your buyers send you wild food orders or do you operate inversely by taking what you forage to the buyers? Basically I send out a newsletter, a kind of information catalogue about what's good, what's in season, what's coming to an end, and what's coming up. Then I get orders and ship them to my customers. That said, nature is always full of surprises! I have learned the preferences of many chefs when foraging and when I find wild foods of particular interest, I send pictures and bag them up based on the orders of the chefs.

Do you occasionally experience difficulties fulfilling orders? There was a time I would run around trying to compensate when nature did not provide what chefs ordered, spending hours searching for what was not there. This is no longer a part of my practice. I offer supplements or alternatives. I pick stuff at its best, and I don't make apologies for nature.

Who was your first customer? My first customer in Copenhagen was Noma, followed by Manfreds, a steady costumer of mine for a long time.

Who are your regular customers? Noma, Amass, AOC, Geranium, Relæ, Barr, Manfreds, Geist, Format, Taller, Molskroen, Alchemist, La Banchina, and Mielcke og Hurtigkarl are some of them.

Is there one wild food you're best known for? I believe I'm known to provide almost all wild foods, at least I would hope so. Watercress, however, is definitely one of the herbs that I have sold in large quantities over the years and, of course, the orange carpenter ant.

THOMAS LAURSEN – *Silkeborg, Denmark*
Forager, founder of *Wildfooding*, published author and Ant Man

Nordlandet | Allinge, Bornholm, Denmark

A short drive over the Øresund Bridge from Copenhagen is the ferry terminal of Ystad, Sweden. Board the ferry and embark upon the chartered 30 nautical miles through the dimly lit Baltic Sea, docking at the Danish island of Bornholm. Adjacent to the jagged rocks at the edge of the northern coastline sits Hotel Nordlandet.

Casper Sundin

– Head chef

I see Nordlandet—or the Northland—as a restaurant with guest rooms, rather than a hotel with a restaurant. It is a place to enjoy the view of the Baltic Sea, to sit in front of a fireplace with a cup of coffee, or to eat a quality meal. It is often seen as a designer hotel but it was not built to exhibit design or to stand out. It is sort of a reinvention of the classical beach hotel, with plenty of fresh air, light, silence, nature, and space to breathe while enjoying food and wine.

All our dishes are based on what Bornholm has to offer: buckthorn from Ibsker, woodruff from Rønne, figs from Gudhjem, and oats from Valsemøllen. All of these ingredients mean a great deal to us. We respect everybody working on Bornholm and we want our cooking to show that. The inspiration usually comes from our visits to local farms, small shops, markets, or walks in the woods or along the beach.

During my career as a cook I learned the classics but also acquired innovative ways of cooking from my time at Søllerød Kro, Formel B, the Bornholm kitchen at Kadeau as well as Stammershalle Badehotel. I try to use a mixture of all these influences in the dishes I create. The food itself is one of my drivers, but creating new dishes will always be my source of inspiration. I find it exciting to watch guests enjoy the flavors of a new dish—in this moment I find new creativity and become inspired as a chef.

Danish lobster in ravioli, lobster bisque, fig leaves, and Jerusalem artichokes

Preparation

Serves 6

JERUSALEM ARTICHOKE
2 artichokes

Peel the artichokes, dice into 1 cm (0.4 in) cubes, and place in water until serving.

LOBSTER BISQUE

4 parsley roots
3 parsnips
1 stem celery
4 onions
3 tbsp tomato puree
lobster shell (from lobster used for ravioli)
3 l / 6 pt water
3 l / 6 pt chicken stock
10 g / 2 tsp coriander seeds
5 stems dill
zest of 2 lemons
6 bay leaves
5 stems parsley
1 1 / 2 pt white wine
300 ml / 1⅓ cup cognac
dollop of cream
pinch of smoked paprika
splash of Pernod

Brown the parsley root, parsnips, celery, and onions in a pan. Add the tomato puree. Then, toast the lobster shells. Put the shells in a gastronorm tray and then into the oven. Toast everything together and then deglaze with the white wine. Add cognac and flambé. Add the water, chicken stock, coriander seeds, dill, lemon zest, bay leaves, and parsley. Bring to a boil and allow 30 minutes to infuse. Strain off the bones and crush them in a Varimixer. Strain the mixture again. Reduce to the desired taste and consistency. Add cream, smoked paprika, and Pernod to taste.

LOBSTER RAVIOLI

10 fresh eggs
30 fresh egg yolks
1600 g / 11 cups type 00 flour
800 g / 5 cups durum flour
75 g / 5 tbsp fine salt
2 kg / 4 lb 6.5 oz lobster, chopped
Jerusalem artichoke puree
dill, chopped

For the pasta dough, hand blend eggs, stir in the flour and salt. Vacuum-pack and let rest for a couple of hours. Take out of the refrigerator at least 2 hours before using to ensure the dough is at room temperature.

For the lobster filling, mix together chopped lobster, Jerusalem artichoke puree (steamed artichokes blended until they have a puree consistency), and chopped dill. Then, roll the pasta dough until you reach a suitable thickness (alternately use a pasta machine). Brush the pasta with egg yolks on the side where the filling is placed and add filling. Fold the other side of the pasta on top and shape the ravioli with your hands. Try and keep the shape of the filling as round as possible while keeping any air out. Then cut out the ravioli into a completely round shape. Place in a tray dusted with durum flour, and let dry in the refrigerator for a couple of hours. Boil for 2–4 minutes, depending on the dryness.

FIG LEAF OIL

100 g / 3.5 oz fig leaves
50 g / 10 tsp grapeseed oil

Blend the leaves and oil for 8 minutes and strain through a cloth.

PLATING

Place the Jerusalem artichoke cubes on the bottom of the plate. Then, add the cooked ravioli on top, followed by the foaming bisque. Finally, add the fig leaf oil.

About the Dish

Bornholm is the only place in Denmark where figs are able to ripen. Using fig leaf oil in this classic lobster bisque with ravioli adds a special Bornholm touch and aroma to a traditional French and Italian dish.

Buckthorn from Ibsker, sheep's milk yogurt sorbet, white chocolate, and oats from Bornholm

Preparation

Serves 6

PICKLED BUCKTHORN

100 ml / ⅓ cup water
100 g / ½ cup sugar
handful of frozen
 buckthorn

Boil a brine of water and sugar. Add the frozen buckthorn. Let infuse over night.

BUCKTHORN PUREE

100 g / 3.5 oz buckthorn
200 ml / ⅞ cup apple juice
sugar
10 g / 2 tsp Citras
14 g / 0.5 oz Gellan
 per liter

Boil the buckthorn with the apple juice. Blend the mixture and strain off the seeds. Add sugar to taste and boil it again with the Citras and Gellan. Let boil for a minute, then let cool. When it is cool, blend to smooth consistency.

SHEEP'S MILK YOGURT SORBET

1.8 l / 7½ cups water
450 ml / 1½ cups
 lemon juice
1 kg / 2 lb 3 oz sugar
250 g / 0.5 pt glucose
8 sheets gelatin
1.75 kg / 4 lb sheep's
 milk yogurt

Boil the water, lemon juice, sugar, and glucose and melt in the softened gelatin. When the mixture has cooled, stir in the yogurt. Then process in an ice-cream machine.

WHITE CHOCOLATE MOUSSE

2 sheets gelatin
700 g / 1.5 lb cream
350 g / 12 oz white
 chocolate

Soften 2 sheets of gelatin. Boil 350 g (0.75 lb) cream and pour it over the white chocolate. Melt in the gelatin. Let the mass cool to about 40°C (100°F). In the meantime, whisk 350 g (0.75 lb) cream until it is airy. Mix it all together. On the plates, form the base of mousse and place to cool in the refrigerator for about 2–3 hours before serving.

OAT CRUMBLE

50 g / 2 oz flour
100 g / ½ cup butter
100 g / ¾ cup oats
 from Bornholm
50 g / 2 oz sugar

Mix together the flour, butter, oats, and sugar and spread on a baking tray. Toast in the oven at 150°C (300°F) until golden.

PLATING

The easiest (and prettiest) way to plate this dish is by looking at the beautiful picture opposite. There are a lot of different elements to plate, so feel free, be creative, and try your own way of doing it to see what looks best to you.

About the Dish

The ability to use ingredients you can harvest yourself is a privilege we enjoy on Bornholm.

Even though we have to go to the other side of the island to find the best buckthorn, it is definitely worth the struggle.

Being able to use your surrounding nature to create a dish based on local ingredients with a particular freshness and acidity coupled with a sweetness and umami that binds it all together, is simply amazing.

Radio | Copenhagen, Zealand, Denmark

When culinary entrepreneur Claus Meyer partnered with close friend and colleague Jesper Kirketerp, restaurant Radio was formed. A product of their synergy, Radio found its place next to the former broadcasting building of Copenhagen. Organic raw materials are sourced from their 2-hectare farm that cultivates 80-plus crops through the seasonal harvests.

Jesper Kirketerp

– Head chef & co-founder

The things that inspire me are quite simple: seasonal produce, nature, my surroundings, and the team at Radio. One of my biggest priorities is using ingredients that are sourced as close to the restaurant as possible, minimizing transport times and ensuring freshness. Danish produce and nature are most important in my creative process. To me, fish and seafood caught in Danish seas are very tasty due to the cold water, and they are best complemented by fruit and vegetables grown in Denmark. I really enjoy involving the team at Radio in the process of choosing different menus, as well as combining ingredients and flavors, because we inspire one another, and use each other's ideas and strengths.

Radio – Copenhagen, Zealand, Denmark

Squid, egg yolk, and Bakskuld

Preparation

Serves 4

LEEKS
4 leeks

Cut off the top and outer layers of the leek. Clean them well to ensure there is no soil left inside the leeks. Then, boil the leeks in salted water until tender.

SQUID
2 squids (300 g / 10.6 oz each)

Remove the head, innards, and ink from the body. Cut the wings off and open the squid by cutting one side open for the squid to lie flat on the table. Roll the squid into a sausage shape, then wrap it in cling wrap and freeze it. When it is frozen, take it out of the freezer, remove the cling wrap, and cut it very thinly (preferably on a meat slicer) while it is still shaped as a sausage.

BAKSKULD

100 g / 3.5 oz bakskuld (salted, smoked, and dried witch flounder)
400 ml / 1¾ cups milk
150 ml / ⅔ cup cream
lemon juice, to taste
salt, to taste
200 g / 7 oz egg whites

Cut the bakskuld into rough pieces to maximize the flavor. Put the bakskuld into a pot with the milk and cream and bring to a boil. When it starts to boil, take the pot off the heat and let it soak for 20 minutes. Then, pour it through a fine strainer. Add lemon juice and salt to taste. Afterwards, stir in egg whites.

EGG YOLKS

2 egg yolks
salt

Salt the egg yolks for a couple of days in the refrigerator. Dry the salted yolks in the oven at 65°C (150°F) for 36 hours.

PLATING

Grill the leeks and cut them into rings. Fry the squid in hot oil but only for a brief moment to prevent it from getting tough. Heat the prepared bakskuld and put it into a siphon. Then, plate the leek and put the fried squid on top. Add the bakskuld siphon next to the leek and finish off by grating the dried egg yolks over the ingredients.

About the Dish

This dish is the perfect image of Radio: a combination of creations by the entire Radio team and inspiration from people connected to the restaurant. When our fish supplier calls to let us know it is now time to use the beautiful Danish squid, the whole team starts dreaming and thinking about squid: what to do with it, how to infuse it with lots of flavor, what kind of texture we want the dish to have, and generally what would be exciting to serve our guests. Then, we move our focus onto the vegetables in season to see how they could best complement the squid as well as reflect the season. What I want the most for our guests is for them to experience the pure and honest flavor of a squid in the sea with "fish friends" and seasonal greens.

STUD!O | Copenhagen, Zealand, Denmark

The Pantone of corroded copper sculptures. The Nyhavn harborside is lit up by the vibrantly restored ferry terminal now known as The Standard, a historical Art Deco building that houses the prized restaurant STUD!O, founded by Claus Meyer. The kitchen of Torsten Vildgaard embodies the Nordic DNA with a menu inspired by nature and a love of experimentation.

Torsten Vildgaard

– Head chef

In everything I do, I work by the mantra: keep testing. During most of my time at Noma, I was hired to experiment, try new ingredients, use new cooking methods—or not cook at all—and to always test the ingredients' expression in terms of their flavor, texture, smell, and appearance. Sometimes I got it right after my first try; but more often it would take me 10–15 attempts over the course of days, weeks, or years before achieving the taste, look, and expression we wanted. I apply this approach to my work at STUD!O. I want to achieve the best possible outcome by testing continually. I encourage my staff to do the same because it is the only way to accomplish greater things. These dishes are the result of hard work and many failures—but in the end, they all represent perfection. They exemplify the result of my mantra—keep testing.

Baked witch flounder with onions and weeds

Preparation

Serves 4

WITCH FLOUNDER

1 skinned witch flounder
salt, to taste
1 stem lemon thyme
10 g / 0.3 oz brown butter

Remove the skirts from the fish with scissors. Cut off the top and bottom of the fish and slice the middle part in two. These pieces form your fish portions. Make sure to save all trimmings for the sauce. Fillet one side of your portions, dip the bones into boiling water for around 10 seconds and brush away the cooked meat with a toothbrush. Open the other side of the fish, while carefully avoiding cutting the fillets off the spine. Remove the bones between the fillet with scissors and line them back up nicely. Salt both sides of the fish portion and refrigerate for 24 hours. Quickly roast the lemon thyme in the brown butter. Smear the fish with the infused butter and put in a sealed container. Bake at 75°C (165°F) for approximately 12 minutes.

TO MAKE THE BUTTER SAUCE

FISH STOCK

1 kg / 2 lb 3 oz witch flounder trimmings
100 g / 3.5 oz white wine
water, to cover

Start with the fish stock. Mix everything in a pot and bring to a boil. Then, turn to minimum heat and infuse for 45 minutes. Strain through a fine-mesh sieve and reduce to around one third of its volume.

REDUCED WHITE WINE

2 l / 8½ cup white wine

Reduce the white wine to one fifteenth of its volume.

SAUCE BASE

300 g / 10.5 oz butter
75 g / 2.5 oz browned butter
75 g / 2.6 oz fish stock
50 g / 1.7 oz reduced white wine
2 egg yolks

Mix everything together except the egg yolks. Bring to a boil and emulsify with a stick blender. Once fully emulsified, add the egg yolks while blending.

FINISHED SAUCE

25 g / 0.9 oz sauce base
3 g / 0.1 oz finely chopped chives
5 g / 0.17 oz pickled ramson capers

Lightly foam the hot sauce and mix with the chives and ramson capers.

COOKED ONIONS

8 small salad onions
125 g / 4.5 oz butter
125 ml / ½ cup water
5 g / 0.17 oz lemon thyme

Cut the bottom off the onions, then cut them in half precisely down the middle. Break into individual cups and remove the membranes from both sides. Mix the water and butter, then bring to a boil. After that, emulsify with a stick blender. Add the lemon thyme and infuse for 30 minutes. Strain through a fine-mesh sieve. Then, cook the onion shells in the boiling butter emulsion for around 20–30 seconds.

PLATING

1 ramson shoot (cooked in lemon thyme butter emulsion for 5 seconds)
2 chickweed
1 yarrow
2 nasturtium
2 sprigs of dill
1 ground elder
1 pink onion flower

Place all the garnishes on top of the baked fish. Serve the sauce on the side.

About the Dish

This dish is the story of an ugly duckling: with some technique and time, an ugly flatfish with a completely crooked skull becomes a beautiful swan, the center of a dish at a Michelin-star restaurant. Our point of departure is one of the cheap - Danish flatfish and we elevate it to a high standard by carving and salting it the day before and using toothbrushes to clean the bones—a transformation so significant that the real innovation, by far, is the end product.

Tartare with pine and toasted rye bread

About the Dish

For this dish, we have looked to the "terroir" of the meat for inspiration. As the meat originates in the pine forest, we smoke and marinate the meat with pine and cover it with a little spruce. In addition, we have spiced the dish with flavors that can balance the pine taste in terms of depth and acidity. With the help of pine, we have tried to create a mood that is meant to give our guests the same feeling we have when we stand in the kitchen and prepare the dish. The smell is extremely stimulating, and we awaken the senses by setting the pine on fire in front of our guests.

Preparation

Serves 4

INFUSED DOUGLAS PINE OIL

33.5 g / 1.2 oz Douglas pine
268 g / 9.5 oz grapeseed oil

Vacuum pack the pine and oil and steam at 80°C (175°F) overnight. Strain through a fine-mesh sieve.

TARTARE WITH PINE OIL

100 g / 3.5 oz venison fillet
20 g / 0.7 oz dried pine needles
8 g / 0.3 oz Douglas pine oil

Lightly freeze the meat. Then, dice the semi-frozen venison into cubes of 5 × 5 mm (0.2 × 0.2 in). Use a smoking gun to lightly smoke the meat with the dried pine needles. Marinate with the oil.

DOUGLAS PINE MAYO

64 g / 2.25 oz egg yolk
24 g / 0.85 oz white wine vinegar
7 g / 0.25 oz salt
260 g / 9.1 oz Douglas pine oil

Add everything but the oil to the Thermomix; spin at medium speed and emulsify with the oil.

BLACK GARLIC PASTE

40 g / 1.5 oz black garlic

Pass the black garlic through a fine-mesh sieve.

TOASTED RYE BREAD

½ loaf rye bread
clarified butter
fine salt

Freeze the rye bread. Slice it on a meat slicer into 1.5 mm (0.06 in) thick pieces. Punch out pieces 6 cm (0.25 in) in diameter with a round ring cutter. Then, line up the rye bread on parchment paper smeared with clarified butter, and season with fine salt. Cover with another piece of parchment paper smeared with clarified butter and bake under pressure for 10 minutes at 180°C (355°F).

PLATING

50 g / 1.75 oz red pine shoots
lemon thyme leaves

Put the marinated meat in the bone and make 5 dots of mayo and black garlic on top. Sprinkle the pine shoots and the lemon thyme leaves on top. Serve on a table napkin with the rye crisp on the side.

Oyster with white currants and söl

Preparation

Serves 4

GILLARDEAU OYSTERS
4 Gillardeau oysters

Open each oyster carefully, pour out any excess juice and check carefully for small pieces of shell. Remove each oyster from shell, cut it in half and put it back into its shell.

WHITE CURRANT JUICE
150 g / 5.25 oz fresh white currants

Juice the white currants, squeeze the remaining juice out of the pulp and pass everything though a fine-mesh sieve.

WHITE CURRANT BOUILLON

**100 g / 3.5 oz white currant juice
70 ml / ⅓ cup filtered water
50/50 simple syrup**

For the finished bouillon, mix the juice and water, and bring to 12 degrees Brix using a refractometer.

SÖL OIL

**60 g / 2 oz dry söl
200 g / 7 oz grapeseed oil**

Blend the söl and oil in a Thermomix at 70°C (160°F) for 7 minutes. Then, pass through a fine-mesh sieve. Stir the oil well before serving, though it should contain a small amount of sediment.

PLATING

**3 frozen white currants
3 small pieces of fresh söl
3–4 purple mustard cress pieces**

Put three pieces of white currants on top of the oyster and cover with the leaves. Pour the juice and oil on top.

About the Dish

The concept with almost all my oyster dishes has been to include a sour berry. Previously we have used green strawberries or different types of currant. The balance between sweet and sour is extremely important because many of my guests have never eaten oyster before, or have tried oyster and not liked it. But given this combination, 99.9 percent end up loving oyster. To give the dish something extra instead of just the white currant juice, we tried using *söl* oil, a red oil derived from a red alga dulse, a type of native seaweed with healing properties eaten over the centuries along the coastlines of the northern Atlantic, namely Iceland. We then discovered shiso—a red herb that really supported the taste of the oyster and used red seaweed, to complement the taste. We had our point of departure in something familiar and used the red color as the common denominator.

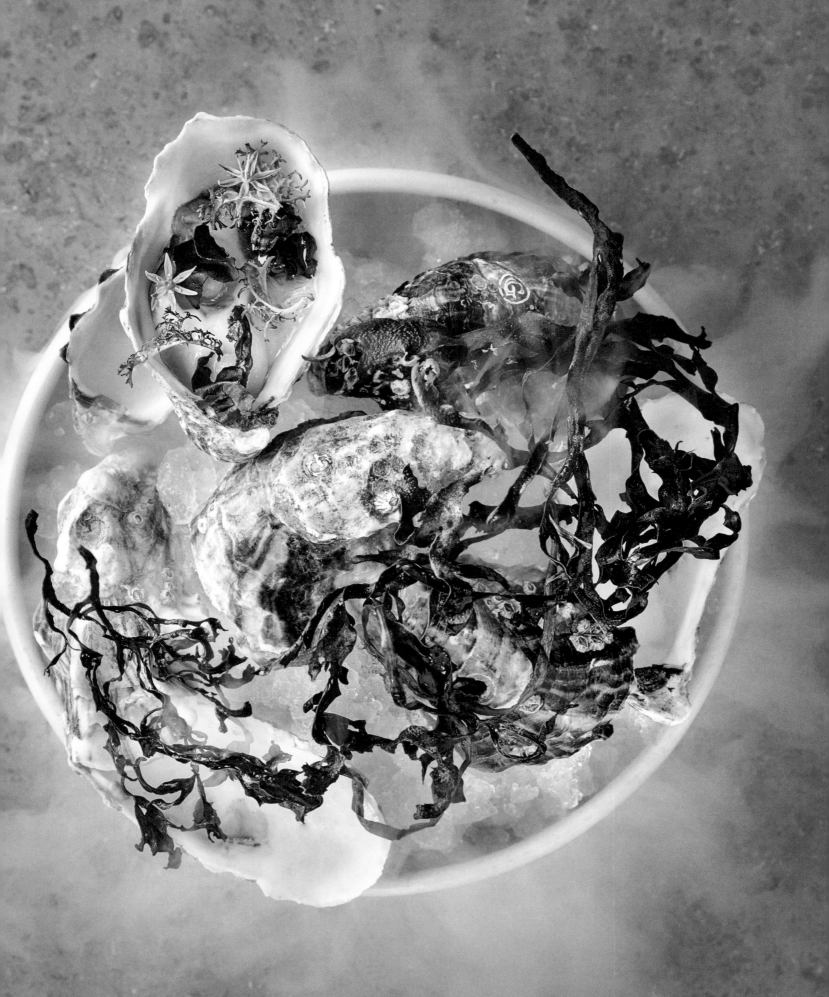

Farm of Ideas
by Christian F. Puglisi

Quality cooking depends on the foods you source, the people behind them, the people you cook for, and the people you cook with. The foods must be sustainable by nature—not only because of the impact on the environment, but also on yourself and everyone else involved.

When I became a father in 2011, I started to understand the way in which cooking was not only the essence of gastronomy but also an act of nourishment, love, and care. I was not only satisfied by serving my son tasty and flavorful food, but I also felt the need to protect him from bad food, from additives, antibiotics, traces of pesticides, and such. As I started to inform myself and see what an outrageous food system so many of us have come to take for granted, I realized that gastronomy could serve as a way out—that the passion for flavor, cooking, restaurants, and hospitality could help spread knowledge and appreciation of good practice in agriculture and farming, and help us better understand nature.

If you connect the dots with a wish to improve the quality of the foods you make, you can create a powerful network that sustains itself with synergies, passion, and vision.

The first realization of that was when we added Manfreds shortly after we opened Relæ. Manfreds was a simpler version of the same core idea of Relæ, namely to serve well-sourced and simply cooked vegetables. The greater volume gave us better ways to source quality produce and educate our staff at the same time. It gave us the opportunity to establish our own wine importing business, Vinikultur, that could connect us directly to the source, acquiring the knowledge to up-skill our staff and ourselves.

An old dream of mine was to have a pizza restaurant—so when the opportunity arose, we opened Bæst, where my love for Italian cooking found a space. While focusing on vegetables and making gastronomy affordable, we had become accustomed to whole-beast butchery and Bæst focused on this new-found expertise. Then we added Mirabelle as our bakery, which not only makes the bread for all our restaurants but also provides a baker's expertise in making the pizza dough. Serving pizza without mozzarella made as little sense as importing it from Italy, so we ventured into producing mozzarella ourselves.

Curiosity, process, and development are what really inspire me. I have always been privileged to have busy restaurants and successful businesses. But I do not believe that it is the result of a certain opportunism, but of a focus on learning something new every day. Bread has inspired me since my earliest days as a chef. When I look back on it now, my original bread recipe was crap and, for the past few years, it has been developed more by the hands of my staff than by my own. But it does not change the fact that I appreciate the results only because I have gone to great lengths to understand the process. The way I have expanded the business has been by creating a business model around the things that sparked my curiosity and what would connect and add value, strength, and synergies to the rest. To me, it would not make sense to hire a baker to bake the bread without participating in the development of both the bread and the bakery, and it is in the same way we established our farm: Farm of Ideas. I believe we can see similar developments in farming and agriculture as we have in cooking and hospitality. I am so inspired to be in this world that literally nourishes us with great produce and makes the restaurants better by improving the quality of our raw materials every day. We started off wanting to grow vegetables carefully for the farm. Along with Lasse, my business partner in the farm, I soon started fantasizing about adding cows that could provide raw milk for the mozzarella production at Bæst. As a result, I now not only think about how to serve or make the cheese, I also think about where the cows should pasture and how to milk them (only once a day for improved quality); what techniques to use to dry their grass to hay; and how to cross-breed them to develop and create our own breed and make the milk truly unique. Once you start digging deeper and combine cooking and agriculture, it allows you to see the world from a different perspective. My love for great food and cooking has never been greater and I intend to keep on digging deeper rather than spreading out with more projects.

CHRISTIAN F. PUGLISI – *Copenhagen, Denmark*
Chef, culinary entrepreneur, and founder of
Relæ restaurant and the Relæ Community

Relæ | Copenhagen, Zealand, Denmark

Just as the dope dealers cleared the cobblestoned streets for the pugs and French bulldogs on what was once the pusher street of Jægersborggade. After the eight pioneering years since Relæ's inception, Christian F. Puglisi placed chef Jonathan Tam at the helm of the kitchen. Over 90% of the kitchen's raw materials are certified organic.

Jonathan Tam

— Head chef

What kind of food do you cook at Relæ? is a question I get asked all the time. Honestly, though I have been here since day one, I am going on my eighth year working with Christian and I still do not know how to answer this question. I have many responses but find it impossible to reduce Relæ down to a few words. My theory of late is that not knowing the answer is precisely what keeps me driven.

We never forced ourselves into a box, but we have set ourselves limitations. As a small team, we had to keep our cooking simple but still wanted to surprise guests; to make things easy to execute but still require a high level of technique. Our dishes have two or three components, often with a vegetable as the main ingredient because we want it to be affordable. We pride ourselves on high-quality ingredients, but rather than importing fancy goods, we started our own farm where we harvest our produce and serve it to our guests the same day. We are constantly cutting away the unnecessary and refining the necessary.

These seeming contradictions have forced us to find creative ways of incorporating all our beliefs and philosophies into our menu. In that sense, we are not theoretical, but pragmatic: we have made a commitment to our guests and chose to become certified organic to have a transparent high standard. Although we had to give up some ingredients we thought we could not live without, in the end we built new relationships with people who shared the same priorities and standards.

As we continue to grow, so do our ideas, which leads to new challenges. Despite all the steps it takes to get to the final dish, we still question every single step of the way. To work with food at Relæ is much more than just cooking.

Relæ – Copenhagen, Zealand, Denmark

Carrot, roasted carrot broth, and lemon thyme

About the Dish

At Relæ, we often like to start with a light vegetable dish at the start of the meal. In the fall, we decided to do a warm starter to give the guests a comforting start.

We feature different varieties and colors of carrots for this dish. Each type has its own distinct taste and texture. The carrots are steamed at 85°C (185°F) for 90 minutes, then they are sliced into thin ribbons. Cooking them this way allows them to become chewy in texture. It would not be the same if we just sliced and blanched them. We believe it is very important to utilize the entire ingredient rather than waste it. We roast off all the trimmings and peel, as though roasting bones for a nice stock. We then take the caramelized carrot and infuse it like tea to get a very intense broth. It actually comes very close to a beef broth, but the dish is completely vegan. At the very end, we add a bit of lemon thyme just to bring out a bit more familiarity, like when you eat a hearty bowl of *pot au feu* flavored with classic French herbs.

Preparation

Serves 4

CARROTS

1 orange carrot
1 white carrot
1 yellow carrot

Peel the carrots and place each one in an individual vacuum bag. Steam the carrots at 85°C (185°F) for 90 minutes. Chill the carrots in ice bath. When the carrots are chilled, slice each one on a meat slicer to a thickness of 1 mm (0.04 in). With the long ribbons of carrots, fold each sheet lengthwise and layer on top of one another. Then cut each set of carrots to a length of 4 cm (1.5 in). Line up the different colored sets of carrots to get a rainbow-like carrot terrine. Place each terrine into the center of a deep bowl.

ROASTED CARROT BROTH

peel and trimmings from the carrots
water
white wine, reduced
5 sprigs of lemon thyme

Place all of the peelings and trimmings from the carrots in a roasting pan. Roast in the oven at 150°C (300°F) for 45 minutes. The edges should be dark brown. Measure the weight of the carrot. You want to heat up water that equals double this weight. When the water is boiling, add the carrots to the water and let steam like a tea for 45 minutes. Strain off the broth, but be sure to squeeze the carrots to extract flavor. Place the strained broth in a pot and season with a bit of reduced wine, add the thyme sprigs, and bring the broth up to a simmer. Then strain off the lemon thyme. Season with salt.

PLATING

Season the carrot terrine with salt and pour the roasted carrot broth table side.

Rye cracker, smoked cod roe emulsion, and steamed brussels sprouts

About the Dish

This snack is a play on a traditional Danish dish of rye bread with butter and smoked cod roe—though the roe is often canned. That's why it is exciting when cod roe is in season because we like to smoke and dry it so we can also use it later. The team wanted to use it fresh, so we brined the cod roe in a 2% salt solution, which firmed up the eggs. Then we hot smoked the roe for a couple of minutes to add some smokiness but leave the eggs raw. We then made a mayonnaise with the smoked cod roe as the only binding agent.

To keep it a light snack, we made thin crisps out of rye bread rather then serving actual rye bread. We got an amazing rye bread baked at our sister bakery Mirabelle, which we blend with some water, spread out really thin, and bake it to get a thin crisp. To balance out the snack, we steam individual brussels sprout leaves and place them on top of the toasted rye bread and smoky cod roe.

This snack is familiar and comforting to local guests and a good way of showing foreign guests a bit of Danish culture.

Preparation

Serves 4

RYE CRACKER

400 g / 14 oz rye bread
400 ml / ⅞ cup water
1.6 g / a pinch of
   xanthan gum

Blend the rye bread, water, and xanthan gum in the Thermomix until smooth. Pass through a tamis. Spread on parchment paper onto trays with a thickness of 2 mm (0.08 in). Bake at 145°C (295°F) for 30 minutes until dry and crispy. Break into small individual pieces roughly 4 × 4 cm (1.5 × 1.5 in) in size.

SMOKED COD ROE
EMULSION

35 g / 1.25 oz smoked
   cod roe
10 ml / 2 tsp cold water
30 g oil / 1 oz oil
10 ml / 2 tsp lemon juice
50 brussels sprout leaves

Start by processing 5 g (1 tsp) of the cod's roe with the water in the Thermomix. It should become smooth and frothy. Emulsify the oil on high speed. It should have the fluffiness and feel of a mayonnaise. Fold in the remainder of the smoked cod roe. Season with lemon juice and salt, and let down with water as necessary. It should just look like eggs barely bound together by the emulsion. Steam the brussels sprout leaves for 10 seconds so they remain green and just cooked. Cool in ice water, then set on paper towel to dry.

PLATING

Pipe cod roe emulsion onto a rye cracker. It should not cover the entire cracker because it will become too heavy and moist. Line up the brussels sprout leaves on top of the cracker, all facing the same direction. In the end, you should have a cracker that looks like a whole cabbage leaf. Spray with lemon juice and season with salt. Serve immediately.

Squid, juniper, and onion broth

About the Dish

Squid is the main ingredient for this dish. When squid, with all its flavor and texture, is cooked properly it is a real delicacy on its own. So we just use some green juniper and onions to support the main ingredient.

This dish is very much about texture. After cleaning the squid we cook it sous vide at 61.5°C (143°F) to tenderize it. In Chinese cooking it is common to score the squid so that it just falls apart when chewed, and we meticulously score both sides of the squid. Green juniper is very strong in Scandinavia but it goes perfectly with seafood. Since it is so aromatic, all we do is crush the green berries with sea salt to season the squid. We take some onions and caramelize them and make a sweet, full-bodied broth. We burn juniper branches over charcoal and add them to the broth to round off the sweetness with some green notes. It is also really nice to smell when you walk into the restaurant.

Preparation

Serves 4

SQUID

1 whole squid, without skin, guts, and tentacles

Vacuum-pack the squid and place in a water bath at 61.5°C (143°F). Cook the squid for 8 minutes, remove from bath, and chill in ice water. Once cold, the squid should be scraped to remove the proteins resulting from cooking. Cut the squid into rectangles of 2 × 6 cm (0.75 × 2.25 in). Then scour each piece of squid with a diamond pattern. This helps tenderize the squid. Reserve the squid for later use.

JUNIPER OIL

**100 g / ⅓ cup oil
30 g / 1 oz green juniper berries
20 g / 0.75 oz green juniper needles**

Blend the oil, juniper berries, and needles at 90°C (195°F) for 9 minutes. Then strain and reserve the oil.

ONION BROTH

**250 g / 8.75 oz onion, julienned
500 ml / 1 pt water
2 juniper branches (length: 15 cm / 6 in)**

Lightly sauté the onions until golden. Add the water and let simmer for 3 hours. After that, set the juniper branches on fire and add to onion broth. Turn the heat off the broth and let infuse with the juniper for 30 minutes. Strain and reserve.

PLATING

Gently sauté the squid in a large pan over medium heat. The goal is to get it to curl slightly without turning golden while still remaining white and translucent. Season the squid with salt and place in the middle of serving bowls. Try to curl the pieces on top of each other to showcase the diamond score. Pour the warm onion broth on the squid and a few drops of the juniper oil. Finish with a few juniper needles on top.

Kødbyens Fiskebar | Copenhagen, Zealand, Denmark

Kødbyen, Copenhagen's meatpacking district, is the cultural pulse of Vesterbro and home to Kødbyens Fiskebar. It's the go-to spot for *frisk fisk*—or fresh fish—in Copenhagen. Think squid, black garlic, pickled pine, and blueberries in the vibrant and energetic open-plan kitchen of chef Jamie Lee.

Jamie Lee
– Head chef

The Nordic Kitchen is an inspiration, not just to me, but also to the many chefs who travel to Copenhagen from all over the world. My inspiration comes from everywhere: the classic French cuisine I was first taught, the changing of seasons, the food markets I walk through when I travel, the people I work with, and the people I travel to meet. Moving to Copenhagen brought a new dimension to my cooking. I learned that recipes could be built from what grows and lives around us. The breadth that foraging, pickling, smoking, and curing gives to our food has shaped the creativity of Fiskebar's kitchen. It is these new ideas and this new style of cooking that drives Fiskebar's creativity and encourages our unique concept and ideas.

It's not over yet. I will continue my endless search for new ideas in an industry that never stops amazing me and never stands still.

Kødbyens Fiskebar – Copenhagen, Zealand, Denmark

Squid, black garlic puree, pickled seaweed, blueberries, and fresh pine shoots

Preparation

Serves 4

SQUID

**340 g / 12 oz squid from
  Denmark's west coast
2 garlic cloves
thyme
tarragon
salt
olive oil
lemon zest**

Cook the squid at 55°C (131°F) for 40–45 minutes in vacuum bags with the garlic, thyme, tarragon, salt, olive oil and lemon zest. When cooked, cut the squid into strips 7 cm (2.7 in) long and 1 cm (0.4 in) wide.

CELERICAC

**1 celeriac
butter
salt
thyme
tarragon**

Cut one celeriac into slices, 6 cm (2.3 in) thick and put in vacuum bags with butter, salt thyme and tarragon. Cook at 80°C (176°F) for 30 minutes. When cooked, cut as the same size as the squid.

BLACK GARLIC PUREE

**1 celeriac
500 g / 17.6 oz cream
500 g / 17.6 oz milk
75 g / 2.6 oz butter
25 g / 0.9 oz squid ink
sherry vinegar
1 fermented garlic clove
salt**

Peel and chop one celeriac into 2 cm (0.8 in) cubes. Boil with the cream and milk. Once cooked, transfer to a blender and blend with the butter, squid ink, sherry vinegar, and fermented garlic. Blend until smooth and season with salt.

BLUEBERRY PICKLED RADISHES

**blueberries
blueberry vinegar
sugar
salt
4 breakfast radishes**

For the pickle, heat the blueberries and simmer for 3 minutes. Take off the heat and press out all the juice. Then in a pot, place 3 parts blueberry juice, 2 parts blueberry vinegar, 1.5 parts sugar and salt for seasoning. Warm and stir until the sugar and salt are blended in. While the liquid is still warm, crudité the radishes into 1 mm (0.04 in) slices and set in the pickle liquid.

PICKLED SEAWEED

**25 g / 0.9 oz pickled
  seaweed
pine infused vinegar**

Julienne the seaweed and vacuum in a pine infused vinegar.

BLUEBERRY POWDER
**500 g / 1 lb 1.6 oz
  freeze-dried blueberries**

Blend freeze dried blueberries into a fine powder.

FRESH BLUEBERRIES
**60 g / 2 oz fresh
  blueberries**

Slice thinly, and use only the inside pieces, not the edges.

PLATING

**20 g / 0.7 oz fresh pine
  shoots
salt
lemon
red oxalis**

Fry the squid with minimal oil, adding the celeriac slices in just before the squid is finished browning. Season the squid with lemon and salt. Garnish the dish with the black garlic puree, seaweed, pickled radishes, blueberry powder and red oxalis. Finally, place the sliced blueberries and fresh pine shoots over the top.

About the Dish

All of our ingredients at Fiskebar are seasonal, which means we rely on the old traditions of pickling, smoking, and curing to fill our winter menus with varied depth in tastes and flavors. I really love working with squid and its texture. It becomes very tender, almost velvety, after 45 minutes of steaming in the oven. It simply breaks down so there is no resistance when you eat it. We then caramelize it in a pan to give it a crisp, golden finish. It is here the flavors collide. Thanks to the sweetness of the blueberries, the richness of the fermented garlic and celeriac puree against the sourness of the pickled seaweed, this dish of seemingly colliding flavors creates a harmonious composition.

Trout with brussels sprouts

About the Dish

Timing is vital in the kitchen. While meat is less delicate and can hold its heat longer, fish can be overcooked in minutes. When we are cooking for 100 or more guests, it is a tight operation and we exhaust ourselves getting it right.

This recipe is really a hymn to local ingredients and sustainable fresh food. We receive the sprouts from a biodynamic farm north of Copenhagen and purchase the trout from a local organic farm. Because of its fantastic quality, the trout only needs to be gently poached in butter and served pink to bring out its best flavor. We serve it with fresh apple to cut through the richness and bind the tastes together with pickled mustard seeds and parsley root puree. Dehydrating the brussels sprouts gives the dish a nutty flavor and crisp finish.

Preparation

Serves 4

PARSLEY ROOT PUREE

500 g / 1 lb 2 oz parsley roots
500 g / 1 pt milk
500 g / 1 pt cream
100 g / 3.5 oz butter
apple cider vinegar
1 lemon, for zesting
pinch of salt

Peel the parsley roots and cut out the core. Cook the rest of the parsley roots in milk and cream. Blend with butter until smooth. Season with salt, apple cider vinegar, and lemon zest. Blend until homogenous.

LOVAGE PUREE

200 g / 7 oz spinach
100 g / 3.5 oz lovage
pinch of salt

Blanch baby spinach and lovage in water. Blend and season with salt.

ONION STOCK

2 shallots
2 star anise pods
40 g / 1.4 oz crown dill

Sweat the shallots and add water to cover. Add the star anise and crown dill. Let simmer for 10–15 minutes and pour off.

CRISPY BRUSSELS SPROUTS

400 g / 14 oz brussels sprouts
butter
salt

Take the leaves off the brussels sprouts, discarding the tough outer layer. Spread half of the leaves on baking parchment with melted butter and salt. Place baking parchment on top and bake under pressure at 150°C (300°F) for around 15 minutes or until golden and crispy. Put in dehydrator for 3–4 hours until completely crisp.

STEAMED BRUSSELS SPROUTS

Steam the remaining parts of the brussels sprouts in onion stock, lemon, butter, and salt.

FRIED APPLE

2 green apples
lemon juice
oil
salt

Dice green apple into 1 cm (0.4 in) cubes, and keep them in water with lemon juice. Then fry with a tiny bit of olive oil and season with salt.

MUSHROOMS

100 g / 3.5 oz trumpet mushrooms
butter

Fry trumpet mushrooms in butter.

PICKLED MUSTARD SEEDS

40 g / 8 tsp mustard seeds
20 g / 0.7 oz apple cider vinegar
sugar
salt

Cook mustard seeds in water until soft. Prepare a pickling liquid with apple cider vinegar, sugar, salt, and the liquid from the mustard seeds, and keep them in the pickle container.

PURSLANE
40 g / 8 tsp purslane

Pick, wash, and let dry.

PLATING
90 g / 3.2 oz pan-fried trout from Bisserup
butter
salt
lemon

Poach the trout in butter, making sure it is still pink in the middle. Season with salt and lemon. Place the trout on top of the lovage puree. Then place little dots of parsley root puree over the trout in a line and layer the mushrooms, apples, steamed brussels sprouts, and crispy brussels sprout over the top. Finish by sprinkling with purslane.

Raw shrimp

About the Dish

Naturally, it is essential to use the highest-quality products when serving raw seafood. That is something we prioritize at Fiskebar. April to October, especially in June and July, is a very good time to find small shrimp in our local waters. With their sweet, buttery taste, serving them raw is the only way to do them justice.

For this dish, seasonal vegetables arrive in the morning from a biodynamic farm north of Copenhagen, followed by fresh herbs from our forager Alexander in the afternoon. This process goes hand in hand with Jesper, the fishmonger, who guarantees his seafood is caught inshore and on a small scale. We use heads and shells to make an oil for dressing the shrimp, which maximizes their sweet flavor. We serve the raw shrimp with cabbage puree to enhance their fresh buttery flavor, while the fermented apple gives the shrimp a kick of acidity.

Preparation

Serves 4

SHRIMP

45 g / 1.5 oz shrimp from Kattegat
20 g / 0.7 oz lobster oil

Peel the shrimp. Save their shells and roast at 190°C (375°F) for 10 minutes; then dehydrate and blend with salt. Freeze the shrimp for a minimum of 72 hours at -18°C (-0.4°F). Remove and defrost. Dress with lobster oil (a neutral oil infused with roasted lobster heads and shells). Then season with shrimp shell salt.

CABBAGE PUREE

250 g / 9 oz butter
500 g / 1 pt milk
1 hispi cabbage
pinch of salt

Heat together the butter and milk and butter in a large pot. Chiffonade the cabbage and add to the warm milk mixture. Stir until all cabbage is submerged, then cook until soft. Drain off the liquid and blend with salt until smooth.

TARRAGON PUREE

300 g / 10.5 oz spinach
100 g / 3.5 oz parsley
150 g / 10 tbsp tarragon
100 ml / ½ cup fresh,
  cold water
salt

Blanch spinach, parsley and tarragon. Once the stems are soft, transfer to an ice bath. Once the spinach, parsley and tarragon are cool, squeeze out all of the water. Place in a blender with the water; then salt and blend until smooth.

FERMENTED APPLE DISCS
1 kg / 35 oz Discovery
  apples

Juice 750 g (25 oz) of the apples and aerobically ferment for 10 days. Use a mandolin to slice the remaining apples into 2 mm (0.08 in) thick pieces and cut out circles with a 1.5 cm (0.6 in) ring. Place in the fermented apple juice.

PICKLED KOHLRABI
DISCS AND RINGS

500 g / 1 lb 2 oz kohlrabi
300 ml / 1⅓ cups water
180 g / ¾ cup white wine
  vinegar
120 g / 4 oz sugar
30 g / 1 oz lemon juice
10 g / 0.3 oz olive oil
5 white peppercorns

1 bay leaf
salt
tarragon

Use a mandolin to slice the kohlrabi into 2 mm (0.08 in) thick pieces. Use a 1.5 cm (0.6 in) ring to cut the kohlrabi into perfect circles. Then, use a 1 cm (0.4 in) ring to cut out the middle of the kohlrabi circles. Place the rings in a pickling liquid consisting of the water, white wine vinegar, sugar, salt, tarragon, bay leaf, and white peppercorns. Dress remaining rings in a vinaigrette of lemon, olive oil, and salt.

PICKLED LEEK FLOWERS
  leek flowers

Cut individual leek flowers from the stalk and place in a pickling liquid with the same ratios as the one used for the kohlrabi. Leave them in the pickling liquid overnight.

PLATING

Place the shrimp in a ring on the plate so each head is touching the tail of the next. Spray a circle of tarragon puree inside the shrimp, then fill the remaining inside space with the cabbage puree. Put 5 apple discs and 5 kohlrabi discs standing up on top of the cabbage puree. Then, build a dome with 15 kohlrabi rings on top, while making sure they touch the shrimp all the way around. Finally, place 8 leek flowers on the kohlrabi rings; try not to fill the negative space.

Chef for Change
by Kamilla Seidler

It all started in Meyer's living room. Claus in shorts after a tennis match, initiating us in his vision for his non-profit Melting Pot Foundation and the incredible opportunity to make the world a better place through food. "Can you combat poverty with deliciousness?"

Plans were set for Bolivia. One of the poorest nations in South America, with two million people suffering from hunger, yet a country with a growing economy, vast biodiversity, and a strong local culture, a Latin American Bolivia had great potential. I was consumed with the idea of giving back to society, and it seemed right to test myself and my skills with a cooking school in a completely different environment.

Melting Pot Bolivia was built as a hybrid social–commercial integration model, an ecosystem consisting of four pillars; 1.) Education, as the engine for change in society, empowering individuals and creating pride amongst the people of Bolivia; 2.) Commercial Products and Services, to improve society in the long term by creating commercial initiatives with a social mission. Two inseparable units that build upon each other; 3.) Research and Development, to constantly innovate and move forward as well as to develop the surrounding community; and 4.) Advocacy and Advertisement, to create awareness of the project, promote its values, and inspire others.

A Bolivian Food Manifesto was written and adapted to the local context to serve as a guideline, drawing inspiration from the principles and ideologies formulated in the New Nordic Food Manifesto regarding respect for the producer, chef, consumer, and environment.

With these fundamental values—that reflected the ideologies Noma has embraced in Denmark—Gustu went from being a culinary school and local restaurant in La Paz to being internationally acknowledged for its casual fine dining on Latin America's 50 Best Restaurants list, all within its first year. Suddenly we had a very different thing on our hands.

We realized that for Claus's dream of a Bolivian food movement to become reality, we needed to make a greater impact and to reach more people in their everyday lives. Thus the culinary concept of Manq'a cooking schools was born: a local program of education combined with a cafeteria for the community. Besides being a female chef in a relatively male-dominated environment, I have faced numerous challenges throughout the process; from navigating cultural differences, to handling logistics and learning about new traditions, new products, new cooking methods, and the art of cooking at high altitude. I hadn't really considered the latter to be a problem until I found myself making rice, potatoes, and bread that just wouldn't cook through. It was like being a student again, but this time in front of 30 actual students looking to me for answers.

Until this moment I believed cooking was what drove me, but it turns out that it is in fact the human aspect: the smile on somebody's face, the glimmer of joy in their eye when you tell them that they are improving, and the shy student who ends up becoming a proud sous chef.

Can you change the world through food? Manq'a is growing steadily and recently entered Colombia with plans to expand to other parts of the world. The program is helping young people in some of the poorest areas to become more aware of a healthy diet and to make intelligent food choices. The goal is to combat diabetes and other food- and health-related illnesses in the future.

After five years, all four pillars are sustainable and independently managed by local people. Within just a few years, we have succeeded in drawing national and international attention to the gastronomy of a small country with a low socioeconomic status by using only locally grown produce, making beverage pairings with only Bolivian wines and spirits, and creating a network of food professionals around the world. The outcome of our work is a large group of pro-

fessionally trained and proud people who believe in themselves and in what their country has to offer.

We simply provided the tools to help the people of Bolivia to grow and develop by themselves—a fundamental philosophy that I believe can be adapted to most places in the world.

Right now we are battling a food crisis even though we have a surplus, an overproduction, of food. We need to make sure that producers can make a decent living to provide for their families, that the chef preparing the food takes a stance on food waste and knows how to limit it, and that the consumer is educated about eating a diverse diet that includes plant-based meals and makes use of every part of

the animal instead of just a few. If all of this is implemented with more focus on the origins of our food and how it is grown, then I am sure the world can and will be a better place.

Food, and its use and production, is something that affects us all, and cooking is a daily routine. Therefore it goes without saying that we are responsible for creating a better future by making intelligent food choices. This is my responsibility, not as a chef, but as a citizen of this world.

KAMILLA SEIDLER – *La Paz, Bolivia*
Former head chef at Gustu, named
Latin America's Best Female Chef 2016

Domestic | Aarhus, Jutland, Denmark

Nestled within the sought-after real estate of Mejlgade in the heart of the historic Latin quarter of Aarhus stands restaurant Domestic. As the name suggests, guests feel right at home in the casual setting. Head chefs Morten Frølich Rastad and Christoffer Norton approach the table to discuss the evening's menu.

Christoffer Norton & Morten Frølich Rastad, Ditte Susgaard & Christian Neve

– Founders

One of our main incentives when starting out at Domestic was to work closely with small producers and farmers so we could create simple dishes with high-quality products. We want to offer ingredients that are produced with respect for animal welfare and sustainability—we would not have it any other way. One of the producers is Troldgården, an organic farm that offers very high-quality pork and lamb. They slaughter the animals in their own small slaughterhouse and deliver whole animals to the restaurant—anything else would not make sense to us. Another sustainable practice we spend quite some time doing in our kitchen is fermenting. We like to work with different kinds of fermentation to be able to preserve ingredients that are not available throughout all four seasons of the year. It not only provides us with a great variety of food to chose from, but also makes us appreciate these ingredients—and their manifold complexity—even more.

Domestic – Aarhus, Jutland, Denmark

Organic pork filet, lacto-fermented rhubarb with dried mushrooms, fried hops, garum, and hazelnuts in butter sauce

Preparation

Serves 4

PORK FILET

600 g / 1 lb 5 oz pork filet
200 g / 7 oz pork fat
salt

Cover the pork filet with pork fat at room temperature. Mature it at 5°C (41°F) for 21 days. Brown the pork in a pan and cook it at 85°C (185°F) to core temperature of 60°C (140°F). Season with salt.

LACTO RHUBARB

200 g / 7 oz rhubarb
6 g / 1 tsp salt
10 g / 2 tsp dried
  mushroom powder
brown butter

Vacuum-pack the rhubarb with 3% salt brine and let it ferment at room temperature for 7 days. Then, store it at 5°C (41°F) for 6 months. Heat the rhubarb in brown butter and sprinkle with dried mushroom powder.

HOPS
4 wild hops flowers
  per serving

Fry the hops at 180°C (355°F) for 20 seconds.

GARUM

2 kg / 4 lb 3 oz fresh
  mackerel
400 g / 14 oz salt

Cut the mackerel into smaller pieces and mix it with the salt. Place it in a plastic container and let it ferment at 60°C (140°F) for about 3 months. After fermentation, sieve through a chinois and pasteurize it. Sieve through a Superbag to get rid of the solids in the mixture.

BROWN BUTTER

150 g / 5.3 oz butter
20 g / 0.7 oz garum
20 fresh hazelnuts

Put butter in a small casserole dish and caramelize it. Pour through a chinois and heat gently. Season with the garum and put fresh hazelnuts on top.

PLATING

Cut the pork into 4 big pieces and place 1 piece in the center of each plate. Spread the hops flowers around the plate—some on top of the pork and some around the plate. Place the lacto-fermented rhubarb, sprinkled with dried mushroom powder, a little to the side of the pork. Pour the sauce in the middle of the rhubarb and the pork.

About the Dish

For this dish, we use Troldgården's traditional, old Danish breed of pig and butcher it ourselves. We are very fond of covering the whole filet—or back piece—in pork fat because it creates a more flavorful and tender piece of meat. To balance this flavor, we incorporate lacto-fermented rhubarb combined with a seasoning of homemade garum. Fried wild hops finishes off the dish. Normally, we use hops when we brew our own beer but we discovered that frying it removes some of its bitterness and leaves an aromatic flavor—the perfect contrast to the pork's fattiness.

Musling | Copenhagen, Zealand, Denmark

Across from the food markets of Torvehallerne and the lively Israels Plads
in central Copenhagen, Musling Bistro, run by the founders of Kødbyens Fiskebar,
delivers fresh, sustainable seafood in a bistro setting. Henrik Vibskov stimulates
the senses with the geometric patterns, and abundance of color in the playfully
executed interior design.

Simon Sundby

– Head chef

Here at Musling, we work organically, sustainably, and with respect for nature. Our vegetables come from Birkemosegaard, a biodynamic farm in Sjællands Odde. The fish are caught by line or by means of other sustainable catching methods. Our mussels, which we get from Limfjorden, are also caught in a similar manner. We believe this is the best way to obtain seafood so that in the future we have plenty of resources available. Some chefs are really fortunate to get their vegetables delivered to their doorstep the morning they're picked by the person from whom they ordered. It is only natural to develop a great respect for the raw materials one works with.

Musling – Copenhagen, Zealand, Denmark

Baked cod with kale, green strawberries, mussel sauce, and smoked parsley oil

Preparation

Serves 4

PICKLED GREEN STRAWBERRIES

- **1 kg / 2.2 lbs fresh green strawberries**
- **500 ml / 1 pt apple vinegar**
- **500 ml / 1 pt water**
- **205 g / 7 oz sugar**
- **10 peppercorns**
- **3 bay leaves**

Go buy some green strawberries at your local berry farm if they are in season. Sometimes it's possible to get them in a well-stocked supermarket. Wash and dry the strawberries. Place them in a good Mason jar. Put the vinegar, water, sugar, peppercorns, and bay leaves in a pot and bring it to a boil. Pour the hot liquid over the strawberries so they are covered, and then close the lid right away. Let them rest for at least 1 week before using.

MUSSEL BUTTER SAUCE

- **250 ml / 1⅛ cups mussel stock**
- **200 g / 7.5 oz organic butter**
- **100 g / 3.5 oz organic cream, 38% fat**
- **15 g / 3 tsp apple vinegar**
- **salt, to taste**

Bring the mussel stock to a boil, take it off the flame, and, with a hand mixer or whisk, mix in cold butter and cream. When finished, mix in vinegar and salt to taste.

SMOKED PARSLEY OIL

- **100 g / 3.5 oz dry hay**
- **200 g / 6.7 oz neutral oil**
- **100 g / 3.5 oz parsley leaves**

Put some hay on the bottom of a big pot. Place a bowl with the oil on top. Set the hay on fire and put the lid on the pot, and leave it until it stops smoking. Take the oil and parsley and blend. Keep blending until it starts to get hot and you can see the oil is getting dark green. Strain it through a fine strainer. Put the oil in the refrigerator to cool down.

BAKED COD

- **400 ml / 1¾ cup mussel butter sauce**
- **100 g / 3.5 oz pickled green strawberries**
- **600 g / 1 lb 5 oz cod on-the-bone, sustainably caught**
- **100 g / 3.5 oz salted butter**
- **400 g / 14 oz cavalo nero (or other organic green kale)**
- **100 ml / ⅓ cup parsley oil**
- **salt and pepper**

Preheat your oven to 160°C (320°F). Heat up the mussel butter sauce in a casserole. Cut the strawberries into eight pieces each. Add a pinch of salt and pepper to the fish, and place it in an ovenproof dish with a good knob of butter underneath. Place the fish in the oven for 6–8 minutes. Fry the kale in a pan, making sure it gets a little color, as this adds flavor to the dish, and remember salt and pepper. Now put it in the casserole with the sauce and the parsley oil.

PLATING

Place the cooked cod in a deep plate. Take off the skin. Sprinkle the strawberries over the fish. Now pour over the sauce and kale. Serve it with a good sourdough bread to soak up the extra sauce.

About the Dish

To make food is to be guided by a feeling. It can be one connected to memories of childhood, your mood, or the weather.

This dish comes from a memory of a warm summer evening in Denmark. I had caught a fish from a little boat on the sea. Cabbage and dairy came from the organic farm I grew up on. Simply by cooking it over a bonfire, the result is a dish of juicy fish, roasted cabbage, and the taste of smoke from the fire.

Falsled Kro | Millinge, Funen, Denmark

The idyllic sixteenth-century building, Falsled Kro is surrounded by manicured gardens and lawns; the scent of smoked salmon wafts across the grounds from the smoke house. Located on the island of Funen, known as the "garden of Denmark," the restaurant reflects its bountiful surroundings with its seasonal menu.

Per Hallundbæk

– Head chef

Every day is an exam and the guests are your examiners.

After nine years in Norway, I returned home to the island of Funen and since I was trained in classic French cuisine during my first years as a chef and developed a high level of expertise in it, I was offered a once-in-a-lifetime opportunity to lead Falsled Kro, an iconic and idyllic pearl of Danish gastronomy located on the west coast of Funen.

Following the legacy of the restaurant's legendary former head chef Jean-Louis Lieffroy—whose soul and name were like writing on the walls for nearly four decades—I entered into this new venture with great awe.

Without making any compromises in the quality of our produce—whether it comes from France, Spain, or is locally sourced—I introduced a more Nordic approach by cutting down on heavy and typically French elements such as cream and butter. Thanks to the expansion of our own herb and vegetable gardens—they have grown from 200 to 1,000 square meters (650 to 3,200 square feet) in size—and the practice of foraging in the nature around us, we have become up to 80 percent self-sufficient.

I am driven by the desire to meet and exceed the expectations of our guests. While "the exam" here starts when the cock crows and wakes up the sleeping guests in the morning, there are countless impressions that make up the absolute sensory experience at Falsled Kro on any given day.

Falsled Kro – Millinge, Funen, Denmark

Sea urchin with piment d'Espelette and lemon aromas

Preparation

Serves 4

SEA URCHINS

**12 small live sea urchins
  from Iceland
300 ml / 1⅓ cups cream
100 ml / ½ cup
  mussel stock
1 lime leaf
1 stem lemon grass,
  chopped
3 egg yolks
salt and pepper, to taste
juice and zest of 1 lime
coarse salt**

Cut the bottoms off the 12 sea urchins and gently scrape out and remove the entrails. Clean them completely inside. Mash the rest of the mass through a fine sieve.

Boil the cream, mussel stock, lime leaf, and lemon grass. Let infuse for 10 minutes. Blend it together with the sea urchin, mix, and strain. Then take 200 ml (⅞ cup) of the mixture and blend it with the egg yolks. Season with salt, pepper and the juice and zest of one lime. Save the rest of the mixture for the sauce.

Place the cleansed sea urchins on coarse salt with the hole facing up. Pour the egg yolk mixture into them. Steam them for 15 minutes at 80°C (175°F) until the mass has settled.

PLATING

**piment d'Espelette
(Espelette pepper)
salt and pepper**

Take the remaining mixture and season it with salt and pepper. Blend to a foam and pour it into the stuffed sea urchins. Sprinkle with Piment d'Espelette.

About the Dish

The idea of this dish derives from my time in Norway, where I had direct access to sea urchins. As they are very sensitive animals, sea urchins cannot be transported very far. Furthermore, Mediterranean sea urchins taste of iron since they grow faster in warm waters, whereas Scandinavian sea urchins, affected by the colder climate, grow at a much slower pace. This makes them more delicate and gives them different aromas. I always found a particularly delicious note of citrus in Scandinavian sea urchins, hence my decision to enhance this aroma.

Trumpet-gratinated rabbit back with celery roulade, garlic, sage, and truffle sauce

Preparation

Serves 4

RABBIT BACK

**2 rabbit saddle pieces,
   with kidneys**
**25 g / 1 oz dried trumpet
   mushrooms (edible),
   macerated and chopped**
100 g / 3.5 oz butter
25 g / 5 tsp breadcrumbs
1 egg yolk
browned butter
salt and pepper

Cut the saddle pieces from the rabbit's back, and remove the tissue and tendons. Cut the kidneys off the back and reserve. Roast the filets for 2–3 minutes in browned butter. Let cool.

Mix the trumpet mushrooms, butter, breadcrumbs, and egg yolk, and season with salt and pepper. Spread mixture between 2 pieces of baking paper and roll it out until it is very thin (approximately 2 mm / 0.08 in), then refrigerate. Once cold, cut it and place on top of the rabbit filets. Cook for 3 minutes at 175°C (345°F) before plating.

CELERY ROULADE

1 celery, peeled
2 tbsp tarragon, chopped
2 tbsp parsley, chopped
2 tbsp chervil, chopped

Cut the celery very thinly on a mandolin slicer to get a strip of 1.5 cm (0.6 in). Then boil the celery strip in salted water for approximately 1 minute until it is slightly tender. Place it in ice water, remove, and sprinkle with herbs. Roll the celery into a roulade, wrap in cling wrap, and refrigerate. When cold, cut it into 5 mm (0.2 in) slices and heat in a steam oven before plating.

GARLIC AND SAGE

8 fat garlic cloves
8 sage leaves
oil

Boil the garlic cloves in salted water 5 times. Then marinate them in olive oil. Fry the sage leaves in oil.

TRUFFLE SAUCE

**40 ml / 8 tsp raspberry
   vinegar**
**200 ml / ⅞ cup rabbit
   stock**
50 ml / ¼ cup beef stock
**25 g / 1 oz black truffle,
   chopped**
olive oil
salt and pepper, to taste

Boil down the raspberry vinegar. and add the beef stock and rabbit stock. Boil down until 100 ml (½ cup). Add the chopped truffles. Season with salt and pepper.

PLATING

Roast the rabbit kidneys for approximately 3 minutes and split in half. Place the gratinated rabbit fillet on a plate with the celery roulade next to it. Lay the roasted kidney on top of the celery roulade and pour the truffle sauce around.

About the Dish

If putting rabbit on a menu tends to "divide the sea," then how about rabbit kidneys? I believe most people are not aware of how delicious they are. So whether in our lamb or rabbit dishes, we always serve the kidneys, too.

Since we work with the highest-quality ingredients, it is important to us, in the tradition of Falsled, to present them in their natural form rather than masking them with creative techniques. The guests should be able to see on the plate what they taste from Mother Nature, which is why I have given the kidney a central place on top of the celery. Celery and truffle simply make the perfect couple and, alongside the tender meat of the rabbit, conclude the simple and light pleasure of this dish.

Paustian | Copenhagen, Zealand, Denmark

The dockyards of Nordhavn, the last stop in Copenhagen before embarking a journey through the "whisky belt" of North Zealand, lay claim to Paustian: contemporary Danish cuisine in an immaculately decorated setting—as one would expect when operating within the renowned architecture of Jørn Utzon. Harborside dining for the sophisticated palate.

Henrik Jensen Junker & Chris Ladegaard Jensen

– Owners, restaurant manager & head chef

Henrik Jensen Junker: My curiosity to taste new things, admiration for aesthetics, and desire to seek out new ingredients and cultures has shaped my passion for gastronomy. I have worked with a wide range of talented chefs who have inspired me. I constantly challenge myself to learn. Prémisse, Kong Hans Kælder, as well as living in France as a young chef, provided me with a great deal of knowledge; my time at restaurant Herman has left a great impact on my direction as a chef. Talented chefs like Thomas Herman, Ronny Emborg, and Thomas Parry, to name a few, have continued to inspire me. It was not until I traveled to Central America, Asia, and Africa that I experienced and understood real food culture. This strengthened my understanding of what local food means for the Nordic region: four seasons of produce dictated by our climate. It is both a challenge and an opportunity to create something

unique, I believe that this is why Nordic food found its place amongst the world's top cuisines. As a chef and restaurateur, I feel it is my duty to develop and create inspiration for our local cuisine; otherwise we may lose our own (food) culture. This is what we strive for here at Paustian.

Chris Ladegaard Jensen: I am always trying to improve, day in day out. The beginning was tough, I have had to make sacrifices, but I have learned to immerse myself in the industry. As a young chef, I worked at Henne Kirkeby Kro—led at the time by Allan Poulsen—where I learned what gastronomy is truly about. This was reinforced during my time as a sous-chef at Kong Hans Kælder; I still apply what Thomas Rode—head chef at that time, taught me. As the head chef of my own restaurant, I choose dishes and ingredients I wish to serve. In the end, it is the guest who determines whether or not one has merits as a chef. I want to challenge guests, not provoke them. That is why I make flavorful food they can relate to.

Paustian – Copenhagen, Zealand, Denmark

Danish pork

Preparation

Serves 4

PORK BELLY

**1 free-range Danish
pork belly
herb salt**

Salt the pork with 10 g (2 tsp)
herb salt per kilogram of pork
for 24 hours. Put the pork onto
a tray and place it in the oven
for 8 hours at 75°C (170°F).
Let cool and cut into 4 pieces.
Broil the pork before serving.

ONION PEEL
4 white onions

Peel and bake the white onions for
10 minutes at 160°C (325°F). Slice
in half and brown in a pan over
medium heat. Divide into petals.

PICKLED
LINGONBERRIES AND
RAMSON CAPERS

**200 g / ⅞ cup white
wine vinegar
200 ml / ⅞ cup water
200 g / 7 oz sugar
50 g / 1.7 oz lingonberries
50 g / 1.7 oz ramson
capers**

Pour the white wine vinegar
into a saucepan, then add the
water and sugar. Bring to a boil
and cover the lingonberries
and ramson capers.

SAGO GRAINS
50 g / 1.7 oz sago

Boil the sago until clear.
Strain and rinse thoroughly
under cold water.

THYME OIL

**50 g / 1.7 oz thyme leaves
100 g / ⅓ cup neutral
(rapeseed or grape-
seed) oil
25 g / 1 oz baby spinach**

Blend together all the
ingredients and heat to
maximum of 65°C (150°F);
then strain the oil.

SAUCE

**1 kg / 2 lb 3 oz spare ribs
1 head garlic
2 onions
7 sprigs thyme
100 ml sherry vinegar
1 l / 2 pt chicken stock**

Broil the spare ribs until dark.
Peel the garlic and onion. Cut
into coarse pieces and sauté
until soft. Add sherry vinegar,
thyme sprigs and grilled spare
ribs. Pour in the chicken stock,
and simmer until it has reduced
into a nice consistency. Strain.

WHITE ONION PUREE

**10 white onions
200 ml / ⅞ cup
heavy cream**

Finely dice the onions, and
sauté without letting them
darken. Add the cream and
boil until soft. Strain and
blend into a smooth puree.

PLATING

**bright green herb
hazelnuts**

Place the pork belly on one
side of a hot plate. Place the
onion petals randomly on the
side and fill with onion puree.
Gently sprinkle sago, pickled
lingonberries, and ramson capers
over the dish. Add the sauce
and top off with thyme oil.
Decorate with a bright green
herb and thinly sliced hazelnuts.

About the Dish

Denmark is known for its long tradition
of pork production and consumption.
As one of the world leaders in
sustainable pork production, we have
chosen to make free-range pig the star
of our dish. It is hard to avoid onions
in a pork dish. For that reason, we
have interpreted the onion in two
ways as a tribute to our Danish nature.
We use both wild lingonberries and
ramson capers from our forests. They
not only add acidity to our dish, but
also pay respect to our produce, food
culture and, lastly, to our agriculture.

Danish lamb

Preparation

Serves 4

MEAT AND SAUCE

- **1 head garlic**
- **2 onions**
- **1 leek**
- **130 g / 4.5 oz lamb breast from Vibygård (4 pieces in total)**
- **rapeseed oil**
- **5 sprigs thyme**
- **2 sprigs rosemary**
- **1 1 / 2 pt beet juice**
- **50 ml / 10 tsp sherry vinegar**
- **salt and pepper**

Peel the garlic and onions. Coarsely chop all the vegetables. In a pan, sear the meat and vegetables in rapeseed oil until they are slightly brown. Cover with water and add the herbs. Let it simmer for 4 hours. Take out the lamb and put it under pressure underneath a heavy object. Strain the stock and reduce until 20 ml (0.7 oz) remains. Put the beet juice and sherry vinegar in a pot and reduce until 200 ml (⅞ cup) remains. Add the stock and reduce until the sauce has a slightly thick consistency. Add salt and pepper to taste. Broil the surface to add flavor and texture. Cut the meat into suitable pieces.

PICKLED FIGS

- **50 g / 1.7 oz brown sugar**
- **200 ml / ⅞ cup port wine**
- **4 figs**

Caramelize the brown sugar and add the port wine. Slightly reduce into a light caramel texture and pour over the figs.

GLAZED BEETS

- **4 large beets**
- **1 1 / 2 pt beet juice**
- **salt and pepper**

Boil the beets until they are al dente. Peel their skin and cut into chunks. Reduce the juice until 100 ml (⅓ cup) remains. Add beets and let them glaze in the sauce. Add salt and pepper to taste.

PLATING

Put a piece of lamb onto a hot plate. Gently place the pickled figs and glazed beets randomly around the meat. Pour the reduced sauce over the food and finish it off with a red herb on top.

About the Dish

This dish combines elements from each season, representing our Nordic food culture in the best way. It combines typical winter ingredients— such as beet, which is harvested during the cold months, and lamb breast from Viby farm—with late-summer ingredients, such as the fig, which we preserve by pickling. Broiling the lamb gives the dish a taste of summer that is balanced by the pickled figs, which add acidity and sweetness. We love to serve this dish in March, as both beet and lamb are available and at their best in terms of flavor.

Substans | Aarhus, Jutland, Denmark

Meet the Mammens: René and Louise founded Substans with the desire to source locally grown, seasonal, organic produce and deliver it in a classic yet daring menu. Guests can pair nine or twelve courses with biodynamic wines or a tea-infused juice menu of organic fruit varietals in a playful setting of wood, vibrant décor, and reflective white brick.

René Mammen

– Head chef & co-founder

This morning my daughter fried me an egg and served it with two basil leaves and a slice of lomo (dry-cured pork loin) on top. Egg and basil—yeah, why not? Simple things can inspire you if you are in a good mood and have an open mind.

Substans began with a simple idea: to create an environment where everyone would feel welcome, a haven to enjoy simple, good, and affordable food and wine. While this rather humble idea of sharing our culinary love is rooted deeply inside us, our ambitions and creativity in the kitchen have grown organically since.

Tradition and old-fashioned crafts-manship meet simple innovation. Enter our third dimension and backbone of the kitchen: our "fermentation basement." Here you will find all sorts of pickled, dried, and fermented produce which gives us the extraordinary opportunity to experiment and innovate throughout the seasons.

We pride ourselves on being 90–100% organic, right down to our staff's food. Sure, it has its limitations, but foraging in the nature around us and sourcing the best organic vegetables and animals from local farmers while not being scared of a drop of oil or a pinch of pepper is what I consider luxury.

Substans – Aarhus, Jutland, Denmark

Pie

Preparation

Serves 4

PIE CRUST

150 g / 5.5 oz wheat flour
40 g / 8 tsp barley
8 g / ½ tbsp salt
100 ml / ⅓ cup beer

Knead everything together. Add more flour if the dough is still sticking to the table. Place in the refrigerator for 2 hours. Thinly roll the dough through a pasta machine (setting 5 for medium thickness on ours). Gently place the dough in a small pie dish. Bake for 12 minutes at 175°C (345°F). Let cool.

PIE FILLING

1 cucumber, peeled
1 kohlrabi, peeled
1 large potato for baking, peeled
100 g / 3.5 oz blue mussels, cleaned and steamed
Pickled sea sandwort:
  Pickled in 200ml / ¾ cup apple cider vinegar,
  200 g / ¾ cup sugar boiled together (you can also use fresh sea sandwort)
salt and pepper

Dice the cucumber, kohlrabi, and potato. Blanch the diced potato for 1 minute. Let cool.

Chop the mussels with a large knife and mix with the diced vegetables. Add salt, pepper, and sandwort to taste.

PICKLE JELLO

100 ml / ⅓ cup pickle brine
2 g / a pinch of Gellan

Boil the brine with the gellan. Let cool, then blend until smooth.

SMOKED CREAM CHEESE

200 g / 7 oz smoked cheese
100 ml / ⅓ cup whole milk
1 tsp honey
salt and pepper, to taste

Mix everything together.

PLATING
  glasswort

Fill half a teaspoon of pickle jello at the bottom of the pie crust. Add the filling. Top with the smoked cream cheese. Garnish with some glasswort.

About the Dish

This dish has been with us for quite some time and it is often the first course on the menu, sometimes with squid and at other times with blue mussels. Despite its modest size, it contains a variety of textures and layers of flavors. From its crisp, malty, and bitter crust base to the jello brine with notes of a traditional Danish herring lunch table; from the extra-crisp salad with crunchy kohlrabi, potatoes, and umami from blue mussels to the smoked cream cheese with a hint of honey on top. This dish can do it all and embodies everything Danish.

Pork breast

Preparation

Serves 4

PORK BREAST
**1.2 kg / 2 lb 10 oz
pork breast**

Salt the meat for 24 hours.
Rinse and bake in the oven
for 12 hours at 78°C (172°F).
Let cool. Cut and broil at high
heat right before serving.

LEMON PUREE

**3 lemons
80 g / 5½ tbsp sugar
40 g / 1.5 oz butter**

Zest lemons and blanch the zest
10 times, using fresh water each
time. Squeeze out the lemon
juice and reduce to about half
with the sugar. Blend together
the lemon mixture, zest, and
butter into a lemon puree.

CELERIAC
**1 celeriac
butter**

Bake the whole celeriac with
peel for 3 hours at 100°C
(210°F) until completely tender.
Let cool and break it into
pieces. Pan sear in butter.

PLATING
**tarragon and
beetroot leaves**

Place the pork breast to the right
side of the center on a plate.
Then place the celeriac to its
left and gently dab some lemon
puree on top. Decorate with
tarragon and beetroot leaves
and serve.

About the Dish

A classic staple at Substans. We enjoy
taking a humble piece of meat and
giving it an awful lot of attention, a
mindset that is central to our kitchen.
In this case, we use Danish organic
pork breast—probably intended for
bacon—and enhance it, elevating
it into a delicious piece of protein.

224

Ti Trin Ned | Fredericia, Jutland, Denmark

After ten steps down to the vaulted cellar of the nineteenth-century building you enter the restaurant, the gastronomic universe of Gassner and Gassner, the creative force behind Ti Trin Ned. With bountiful harvests of produce grown at the couple's country home, Ti Trin Ned is truly a reflection of its surroundings, right down to the Hans Wegner chairs.

Mette & Rainer Gassner

– Founders, restaurant manager & head chef

The base and heart of the dishes in our intimate kitchen will always be the vegetables from our garden at Himmerigskov. Feeling the early spring, we long for light, delicate dishes in the restaurant.

When the summer sun shines, we want to create fresh, vibrant, and herbal flavors. In the rainy autumn, we seek to create creamy and cozy dishes.

And in the cold, Danish winter, we celebrate all the cabbage, kale, and other crops still standing in our fields, and the harvested and well-stocked larder from the late summer.

We are fascinated by the idea of authenticity, purity, safety, and the magic of feeling our way. We are taken by surprise, we make mistakes and every year we are just as excited about the very first potatoes, the fragile radishes, the tiny beets, the large, heavily scented bed of herbs, and the late raspberries prolonging the summer into autumn.

The seasons pass through the kitchen of Ti Trin Ned—with the deepest respect for ingredients, taste, and the quality of every choice we make.

We plant and seed, we harvest and gather—and let nature and the season inspire.

Ti Trin Ned – Fredericia, Jutland, Denmark

Grilled white asparagus with poached organic egg, melted Arla Unika Havgus cheese, and Rossini Gold selection caviar

Preparation

Serves 4

GRILLED WHITE ASPARAGUS WITH POACHED ORGANIC EGG

**4 organic hen's eggs
vinegar for the
   poaching water
4 stems white
   asparagus
melted butter
salt**

Poach the egg in simmering water (1 tsp vinegar per liter of water) for 5–6 minutes depending on the freshness of the egg.

While poaching the egg, brush the asparagus with melted butter and grill on a yakitori or any other small grill. Flavor with salt and the asparagus is ready to serve.

FRIED BREAD CRUMBS

**4 slices yesterday's bread
8 tbsp melted butter**

Fry roughly cut bread in butter until crispy.

PLATING

**40 g / 8 tsp Gold caviar
   by Rossini
4 thin squared slices
   of Arla Unika Havgus
   cheese by Tistrup Dairy
fresh chervil**

Cover the egg with a thin slice (1 mm / 0.04 in) of Arla Unika Havgus cheese and let it melt. Decorate the egg with Rossini Gold caviar, fresh chervil, and butter-fried bread crumbs.

About the Dish

With a desire to celebrate asparagus, we searched for and found the components that highlighted the delicate flavors of the perfectly prepared asparagus: the creaminess of the poached egg, the umami of the Arla Unika Havgus cheese, the salty flavors of the mild caviar, and the crispiness of the bread.

Summer onion flavors and Gothenburg organic chicken breast served with reduced chicken stock and ramson oil

Preparation

Serves 4

RAMSON CRÈME

800 ml / 3⅓ cups cream
200 g / 7 oz ramsons
200 g / 7 oz spinach
salt and nutmeg, to taste

Reduce the cream by half and add the spinach and ramson leaves. Heat up and blend until it has a creamy texture. Season with salt and nutmeg.

REDUCED CHICKEN STOCK AND RAMSON OIL

800 ml / 3⅓ cups reduced chicken stock
100 ml / ⅓ cup ramson oil (ramson leaves blended with rapeseed oil)

Boil 100 ml (⅓ cup) chicken stock for 5 minutes, then add ramson oil and the sauce is ready to serve.

GOTHENBURG ORGANIC CHICKEN BREAST
4 chicken breasts

Fry the chicken breast with its skin slowly until the skin is crispy.

ASPARAGUS

4 stems green asparagus
butter

Poach the asparagus in remaining chicken stock and butter.

PLATING

8 ramson leaves
onion cress
ramson flowers
salt

Place the asparagus in the middle and decorate it with the ramson leaves, onion cress and fresh ramson flowers.

Leave a soft quenelle of ramson crème on the right side and place the chicken breast on the left side. Sprinkle with salt.

About the Dish

We wanted to combine the delicate flavors of chicken with early summer greens: in this case, our first ramsons and early onion cress from Himmerigskov.

We were introduced to the organic chicken from Gothenburg and wanted to create a dish that celebrated its fine flavors. We used the fresh, green onion flavors to highlight this.

Blackcurrant, parsnip, and raw licorice sphere

Preparation

Serves 4

PARSNIP ICE CREAM

300 ml / 1⅓ cup cream
300 ml / 1⅓ cup full
   cream milk
140 g / 5 oz sugar
200 ml / ⅞ cup parsnip
   juice (made from
   6 peeled fresh parsnips)
2 sheets gelatin

Heat the cream, milk, and sugar
and add the gelatine. Cool and
add the parsnip juice. Pour the
mixture into ice cream machine
and stop when the consistency
is creamy and airy.

BLACKCURRANT JUICE

250 g / 9 oz blackcurrants
200 ml / ⅞ cups water
50 g / 1.7 oz sugar

Bring all ingredients to a boil and
strain through a fine-mesh sieve.

BLACKCURRANT
SPHERE

250 ml / 1⅛ cup
   blackcurrant juice

4 balloons
400 ml / 1¾ cup
   liquid nitrogen

Pour 60 ml (¼ cup) blackcurrant
juice into each balloon and
blow up to a diameter of
approximately 10 cm (4 in).
Wear safety gloves and roll
the balloon sphere in the
liquid nitrogen.

When the sphere feels like
a firm ball, it is finished. Keep
in the freezer until serving.

PLATING
   raw licorice

When plating, cut a hole with
a diameter of 4 cm (1.5 in) from
the underside of the sphere
and peel off the balloon. Make
a scoop of ice cream, grate a
generous amount of raw licorice
on the ice cream, and cover
with the blackcurrant sphere.

About the Dish

We discovered that parsnip,
blackcurrant, and raw licorice
complemented each other very
well, and wanted to make a simple,
delicate, and refreshing dessert.

The soft, sweet, and creamy
flavors from the parsnip, the tart
and fruity flavors from the
blackcurrant, and the black licorice
make a harmonious synergy.

We like to discover new dessert
ingredients—and in this case it was
the parsnip. We wanted to use the
sweet, almond flavors from the
parsnip in a dessert and make
guests forget they are actually eating
a root vegetable and just enjoy it.

CLOU | Copenhagen, Zealand, Denmark

Caviar and razor clams: "The cured roe we deem not fit for service, is dried to form compressed blocks of caviar and grated to season to taste." As chef Jonathan K. Berntsen states, wine is the primary source of inspiration and creativity for the kitchen. CLOU: an intimate setting, a consistent delivery of distinct quality.

Jonathan K. Berntsen

– Head chef & founder

Deluxe complexity to elegant simplicity, from more is more to less is more—yet caviar and truffle remain. We do not use caviar because it is extravagant, but because it enhances a dish as a whole. We want each element on the plate to become completely indispensable to the dish. Boiled down to the essence.

Our original concept of 58 touch points and 15 minutes for plating has transformed into numerous simpler yet provocative creations. A shift of complexity from our plating to our *mise en place*.

My culinary mission and love affair with Mediterranean cuisine began as I juggled disparate elements gathered from the atmospheric city streets of Bangkok and the breathtaking Côte d'Azur. I was privileged to be mentored by the eminent French chef Christophe Dufau.

Since day one, CLOU has been about the symbiosis of food and wine. In fact, we select the wines before creating the dishes. This devotion to pairing was acknowledged by numerous awards such as those from the Copa Jerez, the most prestigious accolade in food and wine pairing.

I would describe our food at CLOU as classic, mostly French, not too experimental—but with a gigantic twist.

Most of our seafood and vegetables are sourced locally in Denmark, but we are not limited to a particular region. Quality and taste are paramount—for example, lemons from the Amalfi Coast simply taste the best. Period.

Razor clam royale, citrus, Oscietra caviar, and caviar net

About the Dish

This dish reflects our original concept of more is more. First, I made a dish with a royale of razor clams—which is very old-school—aesthetically plated with caviar in the middle. I had all my chefs taste the dish and as they praised it, I asked, "How can we make it even more impressive?" One young French chef responded, "We could create a net of caviar," which was obviously a joke. But that is exactly what we we did. At our caviar farm, which we are fortunate to visit regularly, we discovered a "gold bullion" made of roe that had been discarded—due to their inconsistency in color or size—which are dried, salted, and pressed into a block. This would be the blueprint for our caviar net. This dish has all sorts of textures and consistencies: the royale is fatty and completely soft, the small steamed razor clams are viscous, the toasted poppy seeds are crispy, and the dried caviar net on top is extremely crispy. Finally, the lemon oil adds acidity.

Wine: I pair this dish with the 2016 Zind Humbrecht, "The Wine That Doesn't Exist," Clos Windsbuhl, Alsace, France.

Preparation

Serves 4

RAZOR CLAM ROYALE

40 large live razor clams
1 shallot
2 sprigs thyme
30 g / 2 tbsp butter
100 ml / ½ cup cream
juice from 2 lemons
salt

Open the live razor clams and peel them out of the shell. Remove their "stomach" and rinse the meat. Blanch 10 of the razor clams for 20 seconds, then cool in ice water. Cut them into small pieces and marinate them in a little olive oil.

Slice the shallot finely and peel the leaves off the thyme sprigs. Melt 20 g (1⅓ tbsp) of the butter in a saucepan and sauté the shallot and thyme. Then add the remaining razor clams for approximately 3 minutes. Add the cream and reduce to half its volume; season with salt.

Put the mixture into a blender and blend at high speed (a Thermomix is recommended). Pass the mixture through a fine-mesh sieve and season it again with a little lemon juice.

Mold the mass into 4 wide-rim bowls and make sure there are no air holes in the cream. Cover the dishes with cling wrap to make sure the taste is not affected by the refrigerator and place to cool for minimum of 4 hours. The royale is finished.

TOASTED POPPY SEEDS
20 g / 1⅓ tbsp blue poppy seeds

Toast the blue poppy seeds in a dry pan while constantly stirring until the seeds have a delicious toasted flavor.

LEMON OIL

50 ml / ¼ cup fruity olive oil
lemon juice

Mix the olive oil and remaining lemon juice.

CAVIAR NET

50 g / 3⅓ tbsp dried caviar
20 g / 1 ⅔ tbsp wheat flour
10 g / 2 tsp sugar
10 g / 2 tsp egg whites

Grate the dried caviar into a bowl and mix in the flour and sugar. Melt the rest of the butter and mix it into the mixture with the egg whites at the end. Put the mass into a pastry bag and cut a very small hole in the end. Pipe 4 grid patterns on a silicone baking mat and dry in the oven at 100°C (210°F) for approximately 10 minutes.

Carefully remove the caviar grids while they are still lukewarm.

PLATING
40 g / 2½ tbsp Rossini Oscietra caviar

Pour lemon oil on top of the royale to cover its surface. Evenly sprinkle the toasted poppy seeds over it. Then carefully add the poached razor clams. Arrange the Oscietra caviar as either small portions or as one portion in the center. Finally, neatly place the caviar net on top.

Squid, Iberico pork pluma, chips, and squid ink

About the Dish

I do not believe in signature dishes—as a chef, one must evolve—yet there are some dishes one simply keeps returning to. That is the case with this delicate Mediterranean "squid in its own squid ink" (or *chipirones en su tinta*, as it is originally named in Spanish). The glazed squid is stuffed with fresh black Iberian pig or *pata negra* (Spanish for "black foot"), braised in herbs and red wine, and served with an *aligot*, a French dish of cheese blended into mashed potatoes. We top it off with squid ink and chips, also colored with squid ink. Everything is served on a black plate. A classic dish that we reinvented as our own: rustic, yet extremely dramatic.

Wine: I pair this dish with NV 1730 Oloroso VORS, Álvaro Domecq, Jerez, Spain.

Preparation

Serves 4

CHIPS AND SQUID INK

1 large potato
20 g / 1½ tbsp squid ink
300 ml / 1¼ cups neutral oil
salt

Peel the potato and cut it into small pieces. Boil until completely tender and drain. Blend the potato pieces in a blender with the squid ink. Season the mixture with salt. Spread out a thin layer of the mixture on baking parchment and let it dry for 1 day at room temperature. Break the dried mixture into small pieces and fry them in the neutral oil at 190°C (375°F) until they are fully puffed up.

Lay the chips on absorbent paper and salt them.

SQUID, IBERICO PORK PLUMA

4 squid
3 tbsp olive oil
1 shallot, finely chopped
½ tbsp chopped rosemary
50 g / 1.8 oz celeriac, finely chopped
150 g / 5.5 oz "pluma" (end loin) of Ibérico pork, either minced or cut with the coarse blade of a meat grinder
1 tbsp tomato puree
1 tbsp dark balsamic vinegar
200 ml / 1 cup strong dark chicken stock
zest and juice of 1 lemon
1 tsp smoked paprika
10 g / 2 tsp butter
olive oil, for frying
salt and pepper

Gently rinse the squid and clean the insides. Peel off the thin skin on the outside. Remove the tentacles as well as the beak from the center.

Pour the olive oil in a large pan and sauté the shallot, rosemary, and celeriac. When the shallot is transparent, add the meat and paprika. Roast the elements until the meat has a golden color. Then add the tomato puree. Allow the elements to caramelize with the tomato puree. Then add the balsamic and 100 ml (½ cup) of the chicken stock. Let the chicken stock reduce to make sure it blends with the other elements. Season with lemon zest, salt, and black pepper.

Allow the mixture to cool off. Using a small spoon, fill the squid bodies with the mixture and close them with a skewer or a toothpick.

Brown the butter in a pan. Roast the squid bodies for about 5 minutes until they are golden on all sides. Add the rest of the chicken stock and squid ink to glaze the squid. Just before the black sauce starts sticking to the squid, add the tentacles to the pan. They should only be there about 30 seconds, otherwise they become tough.

PLATING

Assemble this black and dramatic dish on a black plate with the squid body and tentacles in continuation of each other and lay the black chips on top.

Kokkeriet | Copenhagen, Zealand, Denmark

The large glass façades of Kokkeriet, situated between the manicured Kings Garden and the famous Nyboder district, allow passersby to witness the daily *mise en place* of its open-plan kitchen. The restaurant offers a modern interpretation of traditional Danish cooking served with intricate precision in a contemporary, yet classic setting.

David Johansen

— Head chef

Our inspiration stems from one question: Why can't you turn a local kitchen into a restaurant serving top-tier cuisine? The Nordic kitchen is based on ingredients from the Nordic region and nothing more. Our kitchen is Danish—in its taste, expression, and choice of ingredients. Using Danish cuisine as inspiration, we add another layer that we carefully pair with memories and familiarity. Food creates bonds and relationships; it is around food that we gather with our loved ones. With that as our approach, we have the only menu of purely Danish food on a Michelin level.

Kokkeriet – Copenhagen, Zealand, Denmark

Scallops in brussels sprouts with mussel cream, and pear puree with lemon verbena

Preparation

Serves 4

SCALLOPS IN BRUSSELS SPROUTS

8 brussels sprouts
4 scallops
½ tsp lemon verbena, chopped
1 tsp lemon zest, grated
a pinch of salt and pepper

Separate brussels sprouts into leaves and blanch for 1 minute in lightly salted water. Cool in ice water. Then, chop the scallops into a fine tartare and add the lemon verbena, lemon zest, and salt and pepper to taste. Drip dry the blanched leaves on paper, then fold them together with the tartare inside, shaping them to resemble brussels sprouts again. Steam the stuffed leaves for about 2 minutes before serving.

MUSSEL CREAM SPLIT WITH VERBENA OIL

1 kg / 2 lb 3 oz blue mussels
100 ml / ⅓ cup white wine
1 onion, chopped
1 clove garlic
500 ml / 1 pt cream
lemon juice
100 g / ⅓ cup neutral oil
100 g / ⅓ cup fresh lemon verbena
a pinch of salt and pepper

Clean the blue mussels. Steam with the white wine, onions, and garlic, keeping the lid on. Strain the liquid and reduce. Then, boil the cream until thick and mix in with the reduced mussel liquid. Add the lemon juice, salt, and pepper to taste. Afterward, blend the fresh verbena and oil into a smooth green oil and strain. When serving, the warm mussel cream will split the verbena oil.

PEAR PUREE

3 pears, peeled and diced
juice from ½ a lemon
50 ml / ¼ cup water
1 tbsp sugar
1 tbsp chopped lemon verbena

Mix all the ingredients and steam with the lid on until completely tender. Blend into a smooth puree. Keep warm until serving.

PLATING
dried lemon verbena powder

Start with a smear of pear puree on the plate. Place a steamed, scallop-stuffed brussels sprout on top. Serve with the warm and split mussel cream. Sprinkle with dried lemon verbena powder.

About the Dish

This dish is inspired by stewed cabbage, which is traditionally used as a garnish for meat, whereas the light version we make is a great match for molluscs. Combining the brussels sprouts' bitterness with the sweetness of the pear, the mineral flavors of the scallops, and the acidity of the lemon verbena, creates a well-balanced, pure, and complete taste spectrum. Each ingredient is given their own time on the palate to elegantly reflect the original version and the climate in which we live.

Zander and grilled carrot with yellow peas, pine vinegar, and browned butter

Preparation

Serves 4

ZANDER AND GRILLED CARROT

125 g / 4.5 oz zander (salted with 10 g salt per kilogram)
4 small carrots, peeled and washed
a pinch of salt and pepper

Cut the zander into thin slices. Grill the carrots until lightly tender, then let them cool. Fold the slices around the carrots and steam for about a minute right before serving.

YELLOW PEA PUREE

100 g / 3.5 oz yellow peas, soaked
500 ml / 1 pt chicken stock
1 onion, chopped
1 clove garlic
1 cheesecloth with thyme, black pepper, and bay leaves
50 g / ¼ cup butter
a pinch of salt and pepper
apple vinegar for seasoning

Boil the soaked peas until tender in chicken stock with herbs and aromatics. Strain the liquid.

Add the butter, onion and garlic and blend into a fine puree. Season with salt, pepper, and and apple vinegar to taste. Keep warm until serving.

PINE VINEGAR AND BROWNED BUTTER SAUCE

50 ml / ¼ cup warm and strong, flavorful chicken stock
100 g / 3.5 oz browned butter
50 g / 1.8 oz cold butter
2 tbsp pine vinegar
salt and pepper

Mix the stock, browned butter, and pine vinegar. Blend it with the cold butter until homogenous. Keep warm until serving it.

PLATING

12 nasturtium leaves
12 thyme shoots
1 scallion, finely chopped

Neatly place pea puree on the plate. Place the steamed, fish-wrapped carrot on top. Garnish with nasturtium leaves, thyme shoots and scallion. Serve with the warm pine vinegar and browned butter sauce.

About the Dish

This dish is based on the story of a farmer returning home from a hard day's work in the field. Traditionally, yellow peas are a staple in a Danish farmer's diet, and are often served with salted or smoked meat. However, inspired by the neighboring lake from my childhood, I chose to combine them with freshwater fish. To me, it adds a pure and elegant taste dimension by serving the heavy pea puree with fish rather than meat. It all makes sense naturally when you look to Danish nature: fish from the lakes, pine from the forests, and peas from the field.

Danish lemon mousse with licorice meringues and sorrel sorbet

Preparation

Serves 4

MOUSSE OF GRILLED LEMONS

**150 ml / ⅔ cup juice
from grilled lemons
100 g / 3.5 oz sugar
1 egg
1 egg yolk
4 sheets gelatin,
soaked
350 ml / 1½ cup lightly
whisked cream**

Boil the grilled lemon juice
with sugar. Emulsify into
a thick cream with the egg
and egg yolk. Add the gelatin
and mix with the cream.
Cool the mousse overnight.

SORREL SORBET

**500 ml / 1 pt apple juice
50 g / 1.7 oz sugar
35 g / 1.2 oz glucose
1 sheet of gelatin, soaked
4 bundles fresh sorrel
juice of 1 lemon**

Boil the apple juice with the
sugar and glucose. Add the
gelatin. Cool the mixture to
40°C (100°F) and blend with
the sorrel. Add lemon juice
to taste and then strain. Process
in an ice cream machine.

LICORICE MERINGUE

**50 g / 1.7 oz powdered
sugar
40 g / 1.4 oz egg whites
½ tsp grated raw licorice
½ tsp black food coloring**

Whisk the powdered sugar
and egg whites until mixture
can stand on its own. Add
licorice to taste, then add
food coloring. Afterwards,
spread the meringue out
into a thin layer and dehydrate
overnight in the oven at
80°C (175°F).

PLATING
fresh bronze fennel

Arrange the lemon mousse
into small dots and decorate
with bronze fennel. Add
the sorbet and cover
everything with flakes of
crispy meringue.

About the Dish

This dessert is perhaps one of the
most well-known Danish desserts.
While the original can be quite
heavy, the balance between the
acidity of the lemons, the fattiness
of the cream, and the green
nuance of the sorrel in our version
creates a pleasant taste experience.
We chose licorice because it is
a traditional Danish ingredient
and a taste commonly associated
with Denmark.

Dragsholm Slot | Odsherred, Zealand, Denmark

Our invitation read: "It would be great if you could visit the castle in early Danish autumn because that's when Claus will start cooking with freshly harvested hemp." Invitation accepted, we met Claus in the hemp field at first light. Nestled in the basement of a thirteenth-century castle, Slotskøkkenet is a nature-conscious, sensory dining experience.

Claus Henriksen

– Head chef

Taste, first and foremost. I am inspired by the nature surrounding the castle all year round, which is the main reason I cook with seasonal produce. I believe you should be able to distinguish where you are, the continent, country, region, and season through the food. To me, that's what defines authentic, honest, and clean cooking. That's why I call my kitchen nature-conscious and regional.

I have been very lucky to work with talented, creative, and some would say crazy people over the years. People who have been supportive and inspiring, and who have kept me nimble on my feet. I am grateful for my incredible team and colleagues, and humbled by the castle's 800 years of dramatic history and beautiful landscape, which continues to teach and surprise me on a daily basis. I am constantly finding a wide variety of vegetables and wild herbs with huge potential for use as exciting raw materials. After nine years at the castle, I still feel as if I have just begun exploring the area. There are endless possibilities for how to make use of the nature and our surroundings. Maybe that's why I find the concept of a nature-conscious kitchen so fascinating.

Dragsholm Slot – Odsherred, Zealand, Denmark

Poached oysters with pickled hemp, nuts, and heavy cream

About the Dishes

Arne, one of the local farmers, had been on a business trip to meet with a farmer producing hemp for a Dutch company. The farmer let Arne taste some of the seeds and he was very impressed. For some reason, Arne thought I might find them interesting, and indeed I did! One of the challenges was to find a farmer who would be up for growing hemp. I eventually convinced Søren Wiuff, a sought-after local farmer known for delivering the finest vegetables to several renowned restaurants, to give it a shot. Thanks to my powers of persuasion, he has since established a reputable hemp plantation as a welcome addition to an already fine assortment of produce.

Preparation

Serves 4

HEMP OIL

100 g / 3.5 oz hemp leaves
300 ml / 1⅓ cups grapeseed oil
a pinch of salt

Finely chop the hemp leaves. Then put them in a blender with the grapeseed oil and salt. Blend for about 8 minutes. Strain the oil through a fine bolting cloth or net to be left with the pure oil.

PICKLED HEMP

2 tbsp apple cider vinegar
2 tbsp powdered sugar
20 hemp leaves

Mix the powdered sugar, apple cider vinegar, and cleaned hemp leaves into a vacuum bag, then vacuum-pack the mixture. Let it sit for at least 3 hours.

OYSTERS
4 Limfjord oysters

Gently open the oysters. Strain the liquid into a small pot. Wash the oysters carefully with cold water until shell and impurities are gone. Add them to the small pot with the oyster juice. Just before serving the oysters, slowly warm them over low heat without bringing the water to a boil. They are done when they have retracted a little and are warm.

WALNUTS AND CHESTNUTS

2 chestnuts
4 whole fresh walnuts

Remove the outermost layer of the walnuts and chestnuts. Cut the chestnuts into thin slices.

SEA ROCKET
20 fresh European sea rocket leaves

Wash the sea rocket leaves and let the excess water drip off.

PLATING
100 ml / ⅓ cup heavy cream

Arrange the oysters in 4 small bowls with the walnuts and chestnuts on top. Put a dollop of cream and 1 teaspoon of hemp oil on each oyster. Place 5 pickled hemp leaves on each oyster and garnish with sea rocket leaves.

Warm salad of the day's harvest with fried hemp, blood sausage, and cinnamon cookies

Preparation

Serves 4

CINNAMON COOKIES (BRUNKAGER)

45 g / ⅛ cup golden syrup
65 g / 2.3 oz brown sugar
65 g / 2.3 oz butter
⅔ tsp cinnamon
a pinch of ground cloves
4 g / a pinch of potash
160 g / 5.6 oz wheat flour

Mix the golden syrup, brown sugar, and butter in a pot and bring it to a boil. Add the cinnamon and cloves. Dissolve the potash in a saucepan with some warm water. Once dissolved, stir it into the pot. Then remove the pot from the heat and let cool to around 40°C (104°F). Pour the sugar mixture and flour into a food mixer and mix. Then, remove the dough and split it into two parts. Roll the two parts into dough sausages and wrap them in a piece of parchment paper. Let cool overnight. The next day, cut the dough into thin slices and bake them in a preheated oven at 140°C (284°F) for about 8 minutes.

THE REST

20 small carrots
4 mustard greens
50 g / 1.8 oz arugula
4 tatsoi cabbage
30 g / 1.1 oz hemp leaves
oil and butter, for frying
200 g / 7 oz blood sausage
juice of ½ lemon

Wash the carrots and salad greens thoroughly and let any excess water drip off. Cut the blood sausage into slices or dice it. Heat a skillet over medium heat and add oil. When the skillet is hot, add the hemp leaves and fry until they are crispy. Gently remove them from the skillet. Add the blood sausage to the skillet, toast on both sides, and remove everything from the stove. Add the carrots and salad greens to the skillet, then add a pinch of salt and toast for about 2 minutes. Add the butter and lemon juice. Remove from the heat.

PLATING

100 g / 3.5 oz cinnamon
   cookies
8 nasturtium flowers

Arrange warm salad and carrots on 4 plates. Garnish with blood sausage, grated cinnamon cookies, nasturtium flowers and fried hemp.

Hemp pancakes with unripe apples

Preparation

Makes 12 pancakes

UNRIPE APPLE COMPOTE

4 unripe apples (you can use cooking apples)
2 tbsp sugar
10 g / 2 tsp hemp leaves
1 tbsp oil

Peel the apples, cut them into cubes, and put them in a pot with the sugar, hemp leaves, and oil. With the lid on, slowly bring it to a boil. After it has simmered for 2 minutes, remove from heat, and let cool.

PANCAKES

50 g / 1.8 oz browned butter
150 g / 5.3 oz wheat flour
450 ml / 2 cups milk
3 eggs
½ tsp salt
12 hemp leaves

Melt the browned butter. Put the other ingredients, except the hemp leaves, into a blender and mix together. Then add the browned butter, blend again, and refrigerate. Afterwards, wash the hemp leaves thoroughly and shake off any excess water. Add a tiny piece of butter to a hot pan and pour some pancake batter into the pan. Place a hemp leaf in the center. When the pancake is cooked on one side, flip it and let it cook until golden. When done, remove it and place it on a piece of parchment paper with the hemp leaf on the bottom.

PLATING

Place the pancake in the center of a plate. Spread the apple compote in the middle of the pancake. Then, fold the pancake over the compote into a semicircle. Warm up the pancake in a preheated oven at 100°C (212°F) for about 4 minutes. Serve warm.

108

Copenhagen, Zealand, Denmark

If the Noma team weren't busy crumbing abalone in Australia, leaving the members of 108 to embark on a kitchen take over, we would still be battling the reservations list of the boutique 45-seater to savor the Noma experience. Starting out as a 13-week pop-up in the Noma space, 108 paved the way to its very own permanent address: Strandgade 108 in Christianshavn.

– Head chef & co-founder

Even though I ate a lot of pork roast and boiled potatoes with gravy at my grandma's as a child, I grew up craving flavors different from the ones that dominate Danish cuisine. I was born in South Korea and was adopted when I was four months old. My sister shares the same history and our parents used to take us to Korean gatherings so we could get to know Korean culture and culinary traditions.

My mother taught me to understand and respect the beauty of nature, that food doesn't have to be complicated to be good. She was a skilled cook and always got her ingredients from local farmers. Every year our garden was in full bloom from spring through fall.

When I decided to pursue a career as a chef, I trained in Nordic and French kitchens, which undoubtedly shaped my way of thinking and working, and gave me all the tools I needed to pave my own path. But I realized that what I cook and have cooked in restaurants is very different from what I eat at home—it's much spicier at home.

I always wanted to open my own place, to combine the two worlds. Out of my efforts to figure out how to bring together my memories, what I cook at home, and my professional experiences, 108—or, as we call it, a Copenhagen kitchen—was born. Three pillars form every one of our dishes: foraging, fermentation, and collaborating with farmers. And so far, I think we are taking a path that is very much our own.

108 – Copenhagen, Zealand, Denmark

Raw shrimp with sweet and salted plums marinated with rose oil

About the Dish

We originally created this dish for the HQ dinner of *Gelinaz!* in Brussels in 2017, where we were challenged by Andrea Petrini to remix a deep-fried shrimp recipe by Zayu Hasegawa, chef at Jimbocho in Japan. While working on it, we thought it was important to stay true to our style of cooking but also to be loyal to the recipe as a tribute to the original chef. However, we ended up coming up with something quite different. We opted to use raw shrimp to emphasize the freshness and quality of the main ingredient. We then played with different tones of acidity by adding salted mirabelle plums, fresh physalis, and oxalis leaves, which, in turn, would not only balance the subtle umami sweetness of raw shrimp, but also add a candy-like feature from the dehydrated plums. A bit of seaweed salt adds an extra umami punch. To cut the creaminess of the shrimp, we opted to marinate the tart oxalis leaves in rose oil, creating a sort of vinaigrette that binds the dish together.

Serves 1

SHRIMP

40 g / 1.4 oz raw shrimp from Skagen

Peel the shrimp very carefully to keep the tails intact and remove entire shell. Once they are clean, place them on a sheet of parchment paper and store inside an airtight container in the freezer. Defrost 1 hour before plating.

SHRIMP REDUCTION

100 g / 3.5 oz whole shrimp from Skagen
75 ml / ⅓ cup filtered water

To reduce the shrimp, take the whole shrimp and blitz them with the filtered water in a Thermomix at 60°C (140°F) for 15 minutes at speed 5. Cool it down in a blast freezer. Once cooled, put the shrimp mixture into a vacuum cooking bag and steam at 100°C (212°F) for 1 hour. Strain the liquid through a fine-mesh sieve and reduce to 20 degrees Brix.

PLUMS

1 plum

Wash and dry the plums, and dehydrate them at 60°C (140°F) for 24 hours. Cut them in half, peel them, and slice into pieces of 3 mm (0.1 inch). Cut into triangle shapes. Keep them on a sheet of parchment paper inside an airtight container.

PHYSALIS

1 physalis

Cut physalis in half and then into wedges. Cut each wedge into 3 pieces. Keep the small pieces on a sheet of parchment paper in airtight container in blast freezer.

SALTED MIRABELLE PLUMS

3 g / 0.1 oz salted Mirabelle plums
8% salt brine

Wash and thoroughly dry the fresh Mirabelle plums. Put the plums into a vacuum bag and add 8% salt brine. Seal the bag and refrigerate for at least 6 months. Brunoise the plums and discard the pit. Store in an airtight container.

RED OXALIS LEAVES

1 pot red oxalis
5 g / 1 tsp rose oil

Pick the red oxalis leaves. Brush a sheet of parchment paper with rose oil and lay the red oxalis leaves on top. Store inside airtight container.

LEMON JUICE
1 lemon

Squeeze the lemon and strain the juice through a fine-mesh sieve. Keep in a spray bottle.

PLATING

Put 8 pieces of plum inside a round cutter (ring no. 10) to create a circle. Inside this shape, add the Mirabelle plums, and season with salt and kelp salt. Add 8 physalis pieces inside the circle, and place the shrimp one by one with tails facing inward on top of this base. Then arrange the oxalis leaves with their tips facing outwards around the shrimp as seen in the picture. Season with 5 drops of shrimp reduction, some salt, and a spray of lemon.

Short ribs with grilled onions and smoked butter sauce with elderberry capers

Preparation

Serves 2

MIREPOIX

200 g / 7 oz onions
100 g / 3.5 oz carrots
20 g / 1 tbsp garlic
50 g / ¼ cup rapeseed oil
25 g / 5 tsp lemon thyme

Chop the vegetables and caramelize them in a pot with rapeseed oil and lemon thyme. The vegetables are done when they turn a golden color. Cool down in a blast freezer.

SHORT RIBS

900 g / 1 lb 16 oz short ribs
200 g / 7 oz mirepoix
7 l / 1.5 gal. 7 % salt brine
200 g / 7 oz fermented honey reduction

Portion the ribs into pieces of and soak in the 7 % salt brine for 12 hours. Then, place the meat and mirepoix in vacuum cooking bags, seal the bags, and steam for 12 hours at 90°C (194°F). Cool down in an ice bath for half an hour. Then, heat the ribs in the sealed bag in the oven for 30 minutes at 65°C (149°F). Open the bag and pour the ribs into a pan. Baste with the fermented honey reduction until deeply glazed.

SMOKED CLARIFIED BUTTER

50 g / ¼ cup smoked clarified butter

Cut the clarified butter into pieces and place on a gastronorm tray. Put the tray with butter over another one with ice and smoke over fresh juniper branches for 30 minutes. Store the smoked clarified butter in an airtight container.

PICKLED ELDERBERRY CAPERS

10 g / 2 tsp unripe elderberries
3 g / a pinch of salt
10 g / 2 tsp balsamic apple vinegar

Pick the unripe berries from the stems and wash well. Put the salt and berries into a vacuum bag and seal. Refrigerate for 3 weeks. Then, open the bag, rinse the berries in water, and put the vinegar and berries into a new vacuum bag and seal. Refrigerate for 6 months.

SALTED ELDERFLOWERS

7 g / 0.25 oz elderflowers
21 g / 0.7 oz 6 % salt brine

Put elderflowers and salt brine in a vacuum bag, seal, and refrigerate for at least 3 months.

HORSERADISH JUICE

40 g / 1.4 oz fresh horseradish

Juice the horseradish and pour it through a fine-mesh sieve. Keep the horseradish juice in a squeeze bottle.

ROCKET EMULSION

200 g / 7 oz rocket
20 g / 4 tsp lemon juice
5 g / 1 tsp Dijon mustard
3 g / a pinch of grey salt
200 g / ⅞ cup rapeseed oil
10 g / 2 tsp horseradish juice

Blend rocket with the lemon juice, Dijon mustard, and salt, and emulsify with rapeseed oil. Season with horseradish juice. Pour through a chinois and store in an airtight container. Serve at room temperature.

LEMON JUICE

1 lemon

Squeeze the lemon and pour juice through a chinois. Place and store the lemon juice in a spray bottle.

GRATED HORSERADISH

5 g / 0.18 oz fresh horseradish

Peel and grate another horseradish and keep in an airtight container.

GRILLED ONIONS

100 ml / ½ cup filtered water
1 g / a pinch of dried chamomile
2 white onions
15 g / 3 tsp blackcurrant leaf oil
2 g / a pinch of salt

Bring the water to a boil, turn off flame, add the dried chamomile, and cover with cling wrap, letting the chamomile infuse for 2 minutes. Strain and cool. Peel the onions and cut them in half. Put the onions and chamomile infusion into cooking vacuum bags and steam for 45–60 minutes at 85°C (185°F). The cooking time will vary depending on the size of the onions. Cool down in an ice bath. Grill the onions over oak charcoal; cut every half onion into 4 pieces, and season with blackcurrant leaf oil and salt.

PLATING

elderberry capers
seasonal salad

Warm the smoked butter with a teaspoon of elderberry capers. Place the glazed ribs on a large plate; dress with smoked butter and elderberry capers. For the garnish plates, place rocket emulsion on the bottom, then add the grilled onions. Top with greens, grated horseradish, salted elderflowers, and dress with lemon juice, horseradish juice, blackcurrant leaf oil, and salt.

Rausu Kombu ice cream, toasted barley cream, and blackcurrant wood oil

About the Dish

When we were first researching and developing dishes last year, we quickly agreed that seaweed would be an interesting ingredient for a dessert. I knew that Rausu Kombu once toasted creates light liquorice notes, the decision to develop an ice cream based on that taste came quite naturally. As a compliment to such a rich ice cream, the bitter and nutty note of toasted barley cream, which can faintly resemble dark chocolate, evens out the creaminess. The fruitiness of blackcurrant wood oil adds aroma and rounds this dish perfectly.

Preparation

Serves 1

15 g / 3 tsp koji mole
60 g / 4 tbsp kelp ice cream
5 g / 1 tsp blackcurrant wood oil

BLACKCURRANT WOOD OIL

500 g / 1.10 lb blackcurrant wood, unwashed
1 kg / 35 oz rapeseed oil

Start by smashing the blackcurrant wood with a hammer. Then, put all ingredients into a vacuum bag and vacuum-pack at full power. Put this bag into another and vacuum at 95°C (203°F); afterward place it in the oven at 60°C (140°F) and steam for 4 hours. Cool down in ice and let rest for 24 hours. Strain using a chinois and pack down in 200 ml (7 oz) vacuum bags.

KOJI MOLE

325 g / 11.5 oz toasted koji
500 g / 2 cups 38% fat cream
250 g / 1⅛ cup whole milk
15 g / 1 tbsp birch syrup

Break down koji into unit pieces. Toast in the oven at 160°C (320°F), 80% fan for 1 hour. Remove from the oven. Once cooled, put the toasted koji into an airtight container. Finish by adding the cream. Refrigerate for 12 hours. Put the mixture in the Thermomix with the whole milk. Pass through a tamis with a pastry scraper. Lastly, add 100 ml (½ cup) of this paste to a bowl and add the birch syrup. Then put into 1 litre (2 lb 3.2 oz) vacuum bags.

KELP ICE CREAM

300 g / 1⅓ cup whole milk
150 g / ⅔ cup 38% fat cream
105 g / 3.7 oz pasteurized egg yolks
105 g / 3.7 oz white sugar
3.25 g / a pinch of salt
6.5 g / 1⅓ tsp toasted kelp powder

Put the milk and cream into a pot. Bring to a boil and cool down to 40°C (104°F). In a separate bowl, whisk together the egg, sugar, and salt until sugar is dissolved. Add the dairy mixture and mix well. Then, add to a pot and measure out the kelp powder. Make sure you have plenty of ice available in a separate bowl. Start heating pot without whisking; just stir with a spatula. It is very important that the mixture reaches 82°C (179.6°F). Pour into another bowl over plenty of ice. Add the kelp powder, and make sure it dissolves while cooling it down. Strain through a chinois and leave in the refrigerator for 4 hours. Mix with a hand mixer and pour into Pacojet cups of 600 g (1 lb 5 oz).

PLATING

Put the mole in the middle of a cold plate. Put a round cutter (ring no. 10) around it. Add the ice cream and press with a spoon. Remove the round cutter and spread the oil around the plated elements.

Hærværk | Aarhus, Jutland, Denmark

There are a variety of ways to season a meal, and the team at Hærværk prefer to get their umami boost from grated dried ox heart. The restaurant is owned and operated by four close friends—three of whom are chefs—with a like-minded enthusiasm to serve a deconstructed, experimental daily menu that is firmly anchored in quality, sustainability, and locally sourced ingredients.

Mads Schriver, Asbjørn Munk, Rune Lund Sørensen, and Michael Christensen

– Founders

At Hærværk the whole crew is part of the process, there is no predetermined path. We are not influenced by the past, nor following a future direction; our kitchen is all about adapting to the ingredients available at present.

We create our menu on a weekly basis, taking into account the availability and cycle of seasonal ingredients. Like in the old days, when people needed to prolong the shelf life of their products, we do the same—not for practical reasons, but for taste. We believe that ingredients should be gathered in a way that respects nature. We make a conscious effort to only use fish and crustaceans that have been caught in a sustainable manner and buy only organic meat and vegetables.

When Hærværk first opened, it was about doing everything ourselves, and using the best ingredients. The mix of a zero-compromise attitude, proximity, skills, and intimate relationships with our suppliers enabled us to manifest a deep understanding of the food we make. Our ability to pick and choose suppliers was surely one of the best developments since the restaurant opened. Working with our suppliers demands responsibility on all levels and ensures the perfect ingredients for our guests. This, combined with our knowledge, skills, and constant awareness of the ever-changing landscape, is necessary for creating the Hærværk dining experience.

Hærværk – Aarhus, Jutland, Denmark

Seared Norway lobster with ox heart, pumpkin, endive, and crème fraîche

Preparation

Serves 4

CRÈME FRAÎCHE

100 ml / ½ cup cream
1 tbsp buttermilk
fennel (tops and pollen)

Add the buttermilk to cream and let sit overnight at room temperature. It is done when it has a creamy consistency. Add dried fennel tops and pollen to taste.

NORWAY LOBSTER

4 large Norway lobsters (langoustines)
clarified butter

Clean the Norway lobsters and fry the tails in the clarified butter. The center should only just be touched by the heat.

PUMPKIN AND ENDIVES

½ small pumpkin
200 ml / ⅞ cup apple verjuice
2 endives (preferably green)

Use a mandolin to cut thin slices of the pumpkin, and pickle it in the apple verjuice. Then, blanch the endives in lightly salted water. Stack the endive and pumpkin, then apply light pressure for 30 minutes to form a terrine.

Cut the pumpkin/endive terrine into thin slices and marinate in the apple verjuice, adding Norway lobster coral and brain if available. Season.

DRIED OX HEART

Cover the heart in coarse salt for 2 days. Lightly dilute, smoke in the smoke oven and dry at 8–14°C (46–57°F) until leathery consistency.

PLATING

Arrange the vegetable terrine, Norway lobster, and crème fraîche. Grate the ox heart on top and garnish with fennel tops.

About the Dish

Limited to one per ox, the ox heart is hard to come by and is ordinarily reserved for the lucky few. To bring the ox heart to a wider audience without sacrificing quality, we salt and dry it, which creates an umami boost of smoky flavor and a tough consistency that we like to pair with Norway lobster, bitter salads, and stuffed pumpkin.

Pickled mullet with roe, horseradish, sorrel, and clear mushroom soup

Preparation

Serves 4

CLEAR MUSHROOM SOUP

250 g / 9 oz mushrooms (preferably wild)
75 ml / ⅓ cup stock (fish or poultry)

Lighty salt the mushrooms and infuse in the light stock for 8 hours at 80°C (175°F). Let cool. It can now be frozen. When thawing to achieve a completely clear result, clarify the stock by straining it through a sieve lined with a 100% cotton cheesecloth.

PICKLED MULLET

400 ml / 1¾ cup high-quality vinegar
200 ml / ⅞ cup water
150 g / 5.3 oz sugar
5 leaves lemon verbena
5 leaves melissa
5 lemon grass leaves
1 small mullet, salted

Boil the vinegar, water, and sugar. Infuse the leaves into the mixture. When cold, pour over the salted fish. Then, fillet the fish and lighty salt for 30 minutes. Brush off the excess salt. Afterwards, pickle the fish for at least 2 hours, but no more than 4 hours.

DRIED MULLET ROE

65 g / 2.3 oz dried mullet roe
100 ml / ½ cup 1% salt brine

Place the roe in 1% salt brine overnight. Lightly salt over a period of 3−5 days. Apply light pressure, salt again when everything has been absorbed, and dry in the refrigerator until it reaches the desired consistency.

HORSERADISH

½ root horseradish
50 ml / ¼ cup high-quality vinegar
50 ml / ¼ cup neutral oil

Peel the horseradish and blend with vinegar and oil. This should be done over low heat until you have an airy puree.

PLATING
sorrel

Slice the fish thinly at an angle and place some sorrel on top. Fill with horseradish cream. Flip and fold. Garnish with grated roe. Pour the clear mushroom soup on top at the table.

About the Dish

The fatty, tough consistency of the mullet makes it perfect for pickling. The mullet becomes incredibly tender, and is also reminiscent of oysters. It is an added bonus when the mullet contains roe because it adds a unique depth of flavor.

KOKS | Leynavatn, Faroe Islands, Denmark

In the North Atlantic Ocean, between Denmark and Iceland, lie the Faroe Islands. A hike through the neighboring mountains of Tórshavn brings you to **KOKS** restaurant. Within the intimate setting, a transcendent 17-course tasting menu awaits.

Poul Andrias Ziska

– Head chef

My grandfather, a fisherman from Klaksvík, once visited his oldest son, my uncle, who had moved to the Mediterranean in search of warmer waters. They dined together, and halfway through the elegant meal, my uncle asked:

"Do you know what we are eating?"

"No."

"We are eating squid."

The old man said nothing for a long time.

"I have traveled all the way from the Faroes to visit you and you serve me bait?"

My grandfather had spent much of his life between baiting lines of squid and mackerel in the hopes of a larger catch. How strange for him, then, to finally get out into the world and find himself eating it with fine cutlery.

Though we Faroese have always lived in the middle of a rich larder, we have only recently realized that others may enjoy what we have to offer. We learned to enjoy what we have instead of pining for what is elsewhere. The Faroese landscape is mostly just sea, mountains, sky, and ever-changing light. Rather than learning all the colors of the palette, we are taught to discern a hundred shades of green and blue. We are trained in minimalism, the varieties of the simple.

KOKS has understood the bountiful riches and complexities in the humble language of Faroese ingredients of simplicity and rugged nature—that the tastes of dulse, earth, and air are more deeply rooted in our souls than turmeric, pepper, and butter, and that the rain makes a richer sound than a hundred bells. I wish my grandfather could eat at a restaurant in his own country, put a morsel of its nature into his mouth, close his eyes, chew, and go on an inner journey to taste the earth of which he is made.

By *Faroese musician, composer & singer-songwriter Teitur Lassen*

KOKS – Leynavatn, Faroe Islands, Denmark

KOKS – Leynavatn, Faroe Islands, Denmark

Mahogany clam and smoked cod roe

Preparation

MAHOGANY CLAM
1 mahogany clam

Open and clean the clam. Cut off the tongue (the hard outer section), and cut it into thin slices. Store on a bed of ice in a container in the refrigerator until use. Save the rest of the clam for the puree.

MAHOGANY PUREE

300 g / 10.5 oz mahogany clam
100 ml / 3.5 oz water
100 g / 3.5 oz oil
a pinch of salt

Blend the clam with oil and water until smooth. Season with salt if necessary. Pass through a fine-mesh sieve to get it extra smooth. Keep in a pastry bag and store in refrigerator.

SAUCE

400 g / 14 oz milk
120 g / 4 oz leek
95 g / 3.5 oz potato
40 g / 1.5 oz cauliflower
60 g / 2 oz fish stock
100 g / 3.5 oz salted and smoked cod roe
120 g / 4 oz butter

Put the milk, vegetables, fish stock, and roe in a vacuum bag and seal. Steam the vacuum bag for approximately 30 minutes at 100°C (210°F) until vegetables are cooked. Pour the cooked mixture including the liquid into a blender and mix until smooth. Add the butter. Strain and transfer to a siphon bottle. Keep in a hot box at 60°C (140°F) until use.

DILL VINAIGRETTE

100 g / 3.5 oz dill oil
10 ml / 0.35 oz apple cider vinegar

Mix the two liquids together and keep in a squeeze bottle in the refrigerator.

PLATING

24 small pieces of cauliflower
dried dill powder

Pipe the mahogany puree onto the bottom of the plate. Marinate cauliflower in the dill vinaigrette and add to the plate. Add a spoonful of the mahogany clam slices around the cauliflower. Pipe the warm roe cream on top of everything until just covered. Dust with dill powder.

About the Dish

Working with an animal that is potentially more than 500 years old puts things into perspective: you cannot help but feel like a small dot in an endless universe. Which is why we always show this creature a tremendous amount of respect. When presented with the actual clam, our guests can get as close as possible to the real wonder. Even though the cod sauce and cauliflower create contrasts in flavor and texture, we make sure that the meaty seafood taste of the clam shines through.

Fermented lamb tallow with fermented fish and góðaráð

About the Dish

This is a dish we especially love serving to our guests. *Góðaráð* is a cookie commonly served with coffee or tea in Faroese homes. At KOKS, we replace the sugar with cheese. Since the visual details remain the same, people immediately recognize the cookie when we pair it with *garnatálg*, a sauce made of fermented lamb intestines. Usually we serve it with *ræstur fiskur*, a typical Faroese fish dish. At home, you would get a whole fish, bone-in, boiled potatoes, and *garnatálg*. We have also created an upside-down version of the particular taste of the *garnatálg*. It contains bacteria, which makes it taste quite similar to blue cheese, combined with the cheesy cookie, it resembles a Roquefort. We present the dish in a creamy dressing-like version inside a small cup for our guests to experience the intense flavor. Even though it is a very traditional and common taste, the serving method is very different from what it would be in a Faroese home.

Preparation

CHEESE CRACKERS

250 g / 9 oz cheese, such as Vesterhavsost or any hard cheese like Gruyère or Parmesan
250 g / 1¾ cups flour
50 g / 1.8 oz lactose
4 g / 1 tsp salt
60 ml/ ¼ cup water
100 g / 3.5 oz soft butter

Mix the cheese, flour, lactose, and salt in a mixer. Transfer the mixture to a bowl and add the water and butter. Knead until mass turns into a soft dough. Roll out the dough onto 2 sheets of baking parchment to a thickness of 2 mm (0.08 in). Stamp out the dough using a 3.3 cm (1.3 in) diameter cookie cutter. Bake in a waffle cone iron. Let cool and store in an airtight container.

FERMENTED LAMB TALLOW CREAM

250 g / 9 oz fermented lamb tallow
250 g / 9 oz sour cream
250 g / 9 oz cream cheese

Melt the tallow and roast in a pot for 1 minute. Strain the tallow and let it cool to room temperature. Mix with the cheese and cream and whisk until fluffy. Keep in a pastry bag in the refrigerator.

FERMENTED FISH
1 fermented cod fish

Clean the fish. Seal in a vacuum pack and cook for 20 minutes at 50°C (120°F). Freeze the fish. When frozen, grate it and store in the freezer.

PLATING

Pipe the fermented tallow cream on the cheese cracker. Add the fermented fish. Leave out for 1 minute to let the fish defrost.

Fulmar with beets and rose hips

About the Dish

You can find thousands of recipes for birds and garnishes to pair them with, but you seldom stumble upon a recipe for fulmar. This is one of the challenges of working with Faroese produce: simple food has always been served here, so we are sort of pioneers. That forces us to be creative and work outside the box, at least in the local context. Over the years we have found that the gamey, fishy flavor of the fulmar goes well with the earthiness of beet and the floral flavor of the rose hip. We have used this combination of ingredients in many different variations—this is one of them.

Preparation

THE BIRD

4 pieces fulmar
200 g / 7 oz butter
salt
Sichuan pepper

Cut off the breasts of the fulmar. Season with a little bit of salt on the skin side. Vacuum pack the breast with the butter and cook at 55°C (130°F) in a water bath for 30 minutes. Afterwards, pan fry the breast. Season with salt and Sichuan pepper. Slice and serve.

BURNED BEET
1 large beet

Preheat the oven to 250°C (480°F). Wash the beet and place it in the oven. Bake for 45 minutes, turning it every 5 minutes so it cooks evenly. Remove the burned crust from the beet and cut it into 12 strips 4 cm (1.5 in) in length.

BEETROOT SAUCE

5 g / 1 tsp Sichuan pepper
3 g / ½ tsp rose pepper
200 ml / ¾ cup chicken stock
150 ml / ½ cup beet juice
50 ml / ¼ cup cherry vinegar
2 g / a pinch of salt
2 g / a pinch of sugar

Roast the Sichuan and rose peppers in a hot pan. Add the liquids. Boil, and let infuse for 30 minutes. Strain and season with the sugar and salt.

DEHYDRATED BEET
1 large beet

Peel and boil the beet until tender. Cut the beet into 12 smaller strips, approximately 4 cm (1.5 in) in length. Dehydrate overnight in the oven at 60°C (140°F). Rehydrate the beet in the beet sauce before serving.

BOILED BEET

1 large beet
salted water

Peel and boil the beet until tender in salt water. Cut into 12 smaller strips, approximately 4 cm (1.5 in) in length. Blanch in salt water before serving.

PLATING

pickled rose hip petals
red wood sorrel
ground elder
burned garlic powder

Place the fulmar breast in the center of the plate. Add 3 pieces of each type of beet on the side of the breast so that it forms a half-circle. Place 4 pieces of pickled rose petal on top of the beets. Then cover the beets with wood sorrel and ground elder. Finish by dusting the garnish with burned garlic powder. Pour 2 spoonfuls of the sauce on the garnish when serving.

RECIPES

NORDIC *by* NATURE

BORDERLESS CO. WOULD LIKE TO THANK: Andrea Petrini, Christian F. Puglisi, Lasse Linding, Claus Meyer, Christina Heinze Johansson, Kamilla Seidler, Alex Grazioli, Sumaya Prado, Nordic Food Lab, Mathias Skovmand-Larsen, Roland Rittman, Karin Birgitta Kraft, Thomas Laursen, 108 – Kristian Baumann, Sara de Lemos Macedo, Alchemist – Rasmus Munk, Katja Seerup Clausen, AMASS – Matthew Orlando, Louise Walter Hansen, Christian Alexander Møller Bach, AOC – Søren Selin, Christian Aarø, Kristian Brask Thomsen, BROR – Victor Wågman, Samuel Nutter, CLOU – Jonathan K. Berntsen, Martin Gottlieb Sørensen, Domestic – Morten Frølich Rastad, Christian Neve, Christoffer Norton, Ditte Susgaard, Dragsholm Slot – Claus Henriksen, Christoffer Sørensen, Ursula Rosenkrantz Ugilt, Falsled Kro – Per Hallundbæk, Frederikshøj – Wassim Hallal, Jeppe Lund, Gastromé – Søren Jakobsen, William Jørgensen, Trine Ipsen, Hotel Frederiksminde – Jona Mikkelsen, Hærværk – Michael Christensen, Rune Lund Sørensen, Asbjørn Munk, Mads Schriver, Høst & Vækst – Jonas Christensen, Anders Rytter, Nikolai Lind, Kadeau – Nicolai Nørregaard, Michael Mortensen, Flemming Nørregaard, Lone Hørlyk, Kokkeriet – David Johansen, Buqe Peci, KOKS – Poul Andrias Ziska, Karin Visth, Johannes Jensen, Teitur Lassen, Jens L. Thomsen, Kødbyens Fiskebar – Jamie Lee, Musling – Simon Sundby, No.2 – Nikolaj Køster, Nordlandet – Casper Sundin, Nanna Löwe, Jonas Lemvig Pedersen, Paustian – Henrik Jensen Junker, Chris Ladegaard Jensen, PONY – Lars Lundø Jakobsen, Radio – Jesper Kirketerp, Relæ – Jonathan Tam, Rasmus Bay Arnbjerg, STUD!O – Torsten Vildgaard, Mathias Pachler, Substans – René Mammen, Nick Laursen, Ti Trin Ned – Mette & Rainer Gassner, Ulo – Hotel Arctic – Heine Rynkeby Knudsen, Erik Bjerregaard | Joseph Capé Bernasol, Monique Schröder, Paul Söderberg, Kevin Searle, Post Studio, Maria K. Vous, Peter Falcon-Fernandes, Louise Norup Hellener, Sami Tallberg, Lars Hinnerskov Eriksen, Eva Söderberg, Camilla Jørgensen, Alexandre Papatheodorou, Tue Svane, Jimmy Duus Jensen and Sebastian Wang-Holm

Concept, photography and text by Borderless Co. This book was edited and designed by Gestalten.

Edited by **Robert Klanten**
Contributing Editors: **Borderless Co.** (**Björn Söderberg, Henrik Arild Beierholm Pederson, Joshua Finzel** and **Michael Jepsen**)

Foreword by **Andrea Petrini**
Preface by **Borderless Co.**
Texts and recipes written by **Borderless Co.**
Editorials by **Christian F. Puglisi, Claus Meyer, Roberto Flore & Michael Bom Frøst, Kamilla Seidler, Roland Rittman,** and **Thomas Laursen**

The original measurements (metric) are true to how they have been provided by the chefs and retain their absolute precision. The conversion of the measurements (to imperial) in all recipes has been given based on the information provided and as accurately as possible.

Project Management by **Sam Stevenson**

Design, layout and cover by **Mona Osterkamp**

Typeface: Baskerville by **John Baskerville**

Photography by **Michael Jepsen**
Additional photography by **Alex Grazioli** (p. 186) and **Melting Pot Foundation** (p. 187)

Printed by **Nino Druck GmbH**, Neustadt / Weinstraße
Made in Germany

Published by Gestalten, Berlin 2018
ISBN 978-3-89955-947-7

For more information, and to order books, please visit www.gestalten.com

Bibliographic information published by the Deutsche Nationalbibliothek. The Deutsche Nationalbibliothek lists this publication in the Deutsche National-bibliografie; detailed bibliographic data are available online at www.dnb.d-nb.de

None of the content in this book was published in exchange for payment by commercial parties or designers; Gestalten selected all included work based solely on its artistic merit.

This book was printed on paper certified according to the standards of the FSC®.